THE CHURCHYARDS HANDBOOK

Advice on the history and significance
of churchyards, their care, improvement
and maintenance

*1988 edition
newly revised*

by

PETER BURMAN, FSA

and

THE VERY REV. HENRY STAPLETON, FSA,
DEAN OF CARLISLE

CHURCH HOUSE PUBLISHING
Church House, Great Smith Street, London SW1P 3NZ

ISBN 0 7151 7554 8

Published for the Council for the Care of Churches by
Church House Publishing.
First edition 1962
Second edition 1976
Third edition fully revised and reset 1988

THE EDITORS
Peter Burman is Secretary of the Council for the Care of Churches and
the Cathedrals Advisory Commission for England, and is specially
interested in the history of art and architecture and in the work of the
contemporary artist and craftsman.

Henry Stapleton is a long-serving member of the Council for the Care of
Churches, and following a period as a Canon Residentiary of Rochester
Cathedral, he is now Dean of Carlisle Cathedral. For many years
Secretary of the Diocesan Advisory Committee (York), he also has the
practical experience of a parish priest. As a trustee of the Redundant
Churches Fund, he is actively concerned with the care and conservation
of the churches and churchyards in their care, which collectively are the
size of a small diocese.

Printed in England by Tas Print, George Lane, South Woodford, Essex

Table of Contents

APPENDICES

Notes on Illustrations

Front Cover   The picturesque nineteenth-century lychgate at St Mary Magdalene, Offley, Hertfordshire. Every churchyard should have a properly defined entrance, well-designed and welcoming; nineteenth-century architects were particularly successful at designing lychgates which complement the enclosing walls of the churchyard and the character of the church itself. *Photographer:* Julius Smit

THE MEDIEVAL PERIOD   (All photographs from 1 – 19 inclusive have been taken by Julius Smit)
Plate 1.   Table-tomb at Buckden, St. Mary, in Cambridgeshire – said to be that of the young Duke of Suffolk and his brother, who fled from the plague in 1551 but died of it in Buckden. If that is true, then it is old-fashioned for its date and could easily be of the late fifteenth or early sixteenth century. The sides are richly panelled with gothic tracery, and each of the quatrefoils encloses a shield on which heraldry was probably originally painted.

Following p.32

THE SEVENTEENTH CENTURY
Plate 2.   The churchyard at Burford, St John Baptist, is particularly rich in magnificent tomb sculpture of the seventeenth, eighteenth and (to a lesser extent) the nineteenth centuries. This illustration shows one of the celebrated 'bale tombs' of the early seventeenth century, found chiefly in the district of Burford and only occasionally further afield. This one is particularly interesting because the early seventeenth-century wool bale top has a carved end with a deeply-moving sculptural relief of the Crucifixion, while the base is a twentieth-century replacement

(done uncommonly well) and is a memorial to the brother of John Meade Faulkner, the novelist. *Following p.32*

Plate 3. The use of a headstone as a grave-marker seems to date from the late sixteenth century, but few examples survive before the seventeenth century. Here is a fine group of seventeenth-century headstones at Burford, St John Baptist, Oxfordshire – the one on the left is dated 1697. All three are characterised by their thickness, which is usual for that period. A somewhat heavy-handed and rustic interpretation of baroque style is also character-istic of this period, at any rate in country districts. *Following p.32*

THE EIGHTEENTH CENTURY
Plate 4. This famous headstone at Thursley, St. Michael, Surrey commemorates an unknown sailor but is remarkable not only for its beautiful commemorative verse but also for the relief sculpture showing the murder of the 'unfortunate Sailor', and the names of both the designer and the sculptor are clearly given. *Following p.32*

THE NEO-CLASSICAL PERIOD
Plate 5. All over Europe, the latter part of the eighteenth century and the early nineteenth century were characterised in architec-ture and sculpture by the revival of Greek or Roman styles. This handsome example of a mausoleum-type monument at Thursley, St Michael in Surrey employs the Greek Doric order and, while in the long term the ivy will do it no good, it looks undeniably picturesque. *Following p.32*

THE NINETEENTH CENTURY
Plate 6. These two examples of exceptionally fine lettering on Cornish slate are from the churchyard of St Petroc Minor, Little Petherick, in Cornwall and both date from the 1840s. The one to William Tabb is exceptionally well laid out on the surface of the stone, like a really good title-page to a book; the one to William Cock and other members of his family is less successful in that respect, but more characterful and robust, still employing neo-classical motifs (in the top left-hand and right-hand corners) and with agreeable flourishes and a charming verse. *Following p.32*

good lettering and design in relation to churchyard sculpture. A studio and shop called *Sculptured Memorials* was opened, first at Eric Gill's own studios at North Dean near High Wycombe and then at 67 Ebury Street, London SW1. The headstone illustrated is in the Watts Cemetery at Compton in Surrey, and shows Eric Gill's characteristic thoughtfulness: the traditional shape of a headstone has been subtly modified with a cinquefoiled top and the lettering is beautifully laid out, as on the page of a book.

Following p.32

RANGE OF MATERIALS

Plate 12.　Thanks to Mary Seton Watts, wife of the late Victorian painter G. F. Watts, the hillside cemetery at Compton, near Guildford, is one of the most delightful places of its kind in England. The mortuary chapel was begun in 1896, and its style is Art Nouveau influenced by the Celtic Revival. Much use is made of terracotta, produced in the Compton Pottery founded by Mrs Watts herself; and in the cemetery a number of the grave-markers are themselves of terracotta, like the example illustrated, to Julian Russell Sturgis, d. 1904. The material has weathered remarkably well.

Following p.160

Plate 13.　At Thursley, St Michael, in Surrey is an example of a wooden 'bed board' or 'leaping board' in a style which suggests the early seventeenth century. However, it is a conscious example of revivalism, and is a grave-marker for Una Broxbourne, d. 1911. The beautiful incised verse reads as follows:

> To them that knew her there is vital flame
> In these the simple letters of her name
> To them that knew her not best but said
> So strong a spirit is not of the dead.

Following p.160

Plate 14.　At Hexton, St Faith, Hertfordshire survives a genuine eighteenth-century 'leaping board' with urns as finials on the upright posts.

Following p.160

Plate 15.　At Busbridge, St John the Baptist, in Surrey close to the family graves of the Jekyll family (designed by Sir Edwin Lutyens) is this fine grave-marker of silver-grey oak. consisting of five pieces joined together by wooden pegs (a single piece of oak would not have survived without warping). It is the grave-marker of Francis McLaren MP who died on active service in the Royal Flying Corps in 1917. It has inscriptions on both sides, and survives in very good condition, demonstrating the acceptability of wood as a material for grave-markers in churchyards.

Following p.160

Plate 16. One of the best-loved figures of the late twentieth century, Sir John Betjeman, lies in the churchyard of St Enedoc, at Trebetherick in Cornwall. Sir John Betjeman was a member of the Council for the Care of Churches for many years. His headstone has been executed in slate by Simon Verity, who has taken the development of a flowing script to its ultimate conclusion. The result is one of great vitality and beauty, eminently appropriate to the man commemorated. *Following p.160*

Plate 17. From the eighteenth century onwards (especially in iron-producing counties) iron came to be used as a material for grave-markers. This handsome example is relatively late, com-memorating someone who died in 1871, and is to be found in a quiet corner of the churchyard of St John Baptist, Burford, Oxfordshire. The name of the iron-founder is nearly always to be found on these iron grave-markers and this one was made by Maden of Warminster, Wiltshire. *Following p.160*

THE IMPORTANCE OF NATURAL HISTORY IN THE CHURCHYARD
Plate 18. At Little Barrington, St Peter, in Gloucestershire occurs this fine late medieval tomb-chest datable by the quatrefoil on its long sides. It is notable also for its colonies of lichens and algae, and for the grasses and wild flowers allowed to flourish around its base. *Following p.128*

CONSERVATION IN THE CHURCHYARD
Plate 19. The condition of many fine tomb-chests and grave-markers of other forms is subject to the decay of stone through air pollution and to structural movement. At Little Barrington, St Peter, the conservators Sue and Lawrence Kelland have disman-tled two of the tomb-chests and put them back together again using the correct form of soft lime mortar and non-ferrous metal

cramps to hold the stones together. The illustration shows the work in progress. All over England, our heritage of churchyard sculpture is urgently at risk unless more of such conservation work is carried out by competent practitioners.   *Following p.160*

GOOD NEW DESIGN IN CHURCHYARDS:
COMMEMORATION OF CREMATED ASHES
Plate 20. Plate 21.   At Beckley, the Assumption of the Blessed Virgin Mary, in Oxfordshire the commemoration of cremated ashes has been carried out in a particularly successful way, after much care and forethought. An area of the churchyard is set aside, under faculty, for this purpose close to the church building. On the wall of the church nearby is a tablet in Hopton Wood stone, with lettering by Nicolette Gray, with 'kyrie eleison' (Lord have mercy upon us) in Greek, and in English the text 'Remember in prayer before God those whose ashes are interred in this churchyard'. The same text is repeated inside the church on a framed commemorative panel on which the names of those whose cremated ashes are interred are, from time to time, inscribed. In addition, there appears the following apt quotation from the old Roman Canon: 'Be mindful, O Lord, of thy servants and handmaidens who have gone before us with the sign of faith, and do now rest in the sleep of peace. To them, O Lord, and to all that rest in Christ, grant we beseech Thee, a place of refreshment, light and peace, through Christ our Lord. Amen.' The calligraphy is by Sister Pauline Hall OHP. The mourner has a focus of attention both in the churchyard where the cremated ashes lie, and inside the church, and in the form which is always accessible. We commend this example most warmly.
(Two photographs, one of the tablet and the other of the commemorative panel.) *Photographer:* Nicholas Meyjes.
Following p.112

Plate 22.   Few things are more acutely painful than the death of a small child, and the comfort that a well-designed grave-marker can bring to the parents is incalculable. The sculptor concerned and the parents may have an opportunity, as in other circumstances, of building up a real relationship between artist and client. The commissioning of a tombstone is, after all, the commissioning of a modest work of art. The example illustrated, by Alec Peever, is of stone and the deeply-cut lettering has a welcome freedom about it. *Photographer:* Alec Peever. *Following p.96*

Plate 23. John Skelton, though based in Sussex, has established a nationwide reputation for his work as a sculptor and letter-cutter. Much of his work is to be seen in churchyards, including the illustration on the back cover of the *Churchyards Handbook* and this example in the churchyard of Rainow, Holy Trinity in Cheshire. It is in riven slate and a most attractive feature of it is the contrast between the smooth surface of the inscription panel and the roughened surface of the surrounding area of the headstone. Notice also the quotation from a medieval poem, in Middle English. *Photographer:* John Skelton.   *Following p.96*

Plate 24. The Trustees of the Holst Foundation commissioned from Martin Jennings this headstone for the grave of the composer and writer on music, Imogen Holst, who died 1984. The quotation is from the *Hymn of Jesus* by her father, Gustav Holst. Note the subtly curved shape of the top, and the somewhat attenuated modification of the traditional English headstone shape. *Photographer:* Martin Jennings.   *Following p.96*

Plate 25. The extension to the churchyard at Penn, in Buckinghamshire is widely regarded as one of the most successful achievements of its kind. It is used both for inhumations and for the reverent burial of cremated ashes, and the focal point is the fine cross by local sculptor, Darsie Rawlins, with a Crucifixion carved on one side of the cross-head and the Virgin and Child on the other. The illustration shows the Virgin and Child. It is a fine piece of devotional sculpture, and provides visitors to the churchyard and mourners with a real focus for their attention and their grief. *Photographer:* Julius Smit.   *Following p.96*

Plate 26. The headstone to Gillian von Isenburg, d. 1985, is by Tom Perkins, of Sutton, in Cambridgeshire. Notice again the subtle transformation of the traditional headstone shape. This one is of York stone. *Photographer:* Tom Perkins.   *Following p.96*

Plate 27. Gloucestershire churchyards have been much enriched in recent years by the work of Bryant Fedden, a member of the

Gloucester Diocesan Advisory Committee for the Care of Churches. This one, in the churchyard, at Owlpen, in Gloucestershire commemorates Michael Lewis, d. 1984, who was a lifelong bee-keeper. *Photographer:* Julius Smit. *Following p.96*

Plate 28. Sarah More is one of a considerable number of sculptors and letter-cutters trained at the City and Guilds of London Art School, in Kennington. Her work has a quiet distinction as is shown in this curved-topped headstone to Francis Jackson, d. 1985. *Photographer:* Sarah More. *Following p.96*

Plate 29. A recent headstone in the cemetery at Minehead by Caroline Webb of Edington, Wiltshire, who has made a scholarly study of historic letter forms. This headstone is of Purbeck stone. *Photographer:* Caroline Webb. *Following p.96*

Plate 30. Reynolds Stone, one of the finest engravers and letterers of twentieth-century England, lived in The Old Rectory at Litton Cheney in Dorset. Just over the garden wall from where he lived, in the churchyard, is Michael Harvey's beautiful headstone to him. Notice the revival of two traditional items of churchyard iconography, the motto 'Hic jacet' (here lies), and the weeping willow tree which is an appropriate emblem of mourning. *Photographer:* Michael Harvey. *Following p.96*

Plate 31. Like so many successful late twentieth-century headstones, Richard Kindersley's memorial to Timothy Eckersley, d. 1980, is a subtle modification of traditional shape. The lettering admirably fills the whole space, is beautifully laid out and the last letter of 'Huxley' is given an enjoyable flourish. This headstone is of Welsh slate in the churchyard at Hadlow Down, East Sussex. *Photographer:* Richard Kindersley. *Following p.96*

Plate 32. The commemoration of cremated ashes is a difficult problem, and probably the best solution is a general commemoration as at Beckley in Oxfordshire, illustrated elsewhere. But if a small flat stone is to be provided, then this example by Richard Kindersley in Welsh slate could scarcely be bettered. Notice the use of the whole space available, and the deeply cut and handsome letter forms. *Photographer:* Richard Kindersley. *Following p.96*

Acknowledgements

The editors have received a great deal of help from a working party set up by the CCC, first to consider churchyard memorials, and then to act as a support group for the revision of the *Handbook* as a whole. Its members, in addition to themselves, have been: the Rev. the Worshipful Chancellor Graham Routledge; the Ven. B. R. Marsh, Archdeacon of Northampton; Mr Donald Gunn; Mr David Harte, Faculty of Law, University of Newcastle upon Tyne; Mr A. B. Henwood; Mr Alec Peever; Mr Lionel Wadeson; Mr David Williams and Mr Jonathan Goodchild. In addition to being a member of the working party, Mr David Harte was largely responsible for the recasting and rewriting of the section on 'Legal Considerations', and we are very much indebted to him.

Special thanks are also due to the following: the estate of the late Sir John Betjeman, and the publishers SPCK for permission to quote from *Poems in the Porch;* Hugh Brogan for writing the chapter on 'Epitaphs and Inscriptions'; Mrs Pamela Burgess; Mr Arthur Chater, Botany Department of the British Museum (Natural History); Miss Joan Denne; Miss Eve Dennis, Churches & Conservation Project, The Arthur Rank Centre; Mr Gunnar Godwin; Mr Roy Grant; Mr Richard Grasby; Mrs Francesca Greenoak; Miss Linda Gregory, Yorkshire Wildlife Trust; The Legal Advisory Commission of the General Synod and its Secretary, Mr Brian Hanson; Mr Andrew Heaton, Royal Society for Nature Conservation; Dr Mary Hobbs, Chairman of the CCC Publications Committee; Mr John Dana Josephson; Mr David Kindersley; Mr Jack Laundon, British Lichen Society; Dr R. M. Leaney, The Norfolk Naturalists Trust; Mr Kenneth Lindley; the Rev. the Worshipful Chancellor E. Garth Moore;

Mr Richard Morris, Council for British Archaeology; the Rev. Oscar Muspratt, Rector of Penn, Buckinghamshire; Dr Harold Mytum, for revising and rewriting 'Recording the Churchyard' and Appendix V; Mr F. H. Perring, Royal Society for Nature Conservation; Miss Judith Scott; Miss Janet Seeley, for her help with the Bibliography and Directory of Useful Organisations; the Rev. Brian Shannon, Vicar of Thorpe-le-Soken, Essex; the Rev. Michael Staines, Rector of West Wycombe, Buckinghamshire; Mr Simon Verity; Mr Laurence Whistler.

Part I

The Importance of Churchyards

I

Churchyards – an Introduction

The Care of Churchyards, the precursor of the *Churchyards Handbook,* was first published more than fifty years ago. This is now the third post-war edition of the Handbook and, from our observations of churchyards, it is clear that the principles enunciated over the years have been reflected in action.

Amongst the developments noticed since the previous edition of 1976 has been an increase of interest in headstone inscriptions by local and family historians. The form and decoration of memorials have been increasingly studied and valued by art historians and archaeologists. Nature conservators have seen the churchyard more and more as an ecological area of importance. But above all, perhaps, there has been a revival of a more open interest in the phenomenon of death, both in its macabre associations and in its psychology. Moreover the counselling of the bereaved (or the conscious care of those in the 'grieving process') has become a subject of study for a growing number of people and a whole new professional expertise.

Of special importance in this edition are the new suggested rules for the introduction of memorials into churchyards, and the strong encouragement for commemorating the deceased whose remains have been cremated in Books of Remembrance, which must be adequately designed and housed and properly used. Although we acknowledge the value of memorials associated with cremated remains in the churchyard, we stress the desirability of well-designed and artistic group-memorials, rather than a proliferation of small stones of repetitive design. These recommendations will, we trust, have considerable impact in the years to come.

In the section 'Churchyards – an explanation and manifesto' the previous edition contained paragraphs that have stood the test of time and are reprinted here with very few alterations. Herein is contained a definition and analysis of the nature of the churchyard which is basic to an understanding of what a churchyard really is. Many schemes for 'improvement' fail to appreciate the subtlety of its constituents, with the result that untold damage is done.

We suggest that a churchyard may best be defined as 'the area around a church where the dead are buried'. Topographically, the churchyard is part of the religious landscape as well as being part of the physical and historical landscape; not only is it the setting for the church, but theologically it has a special significance which was particularly well expressed by the late Bishop Healey, in an address to the Royal Society of Arts in 1967:

> Each is incomplete without the other. They are sacramentals; outward and visible forms of the ministering of God's grace to the whole man, who is born, lives and dies, after the order of his creation: and after the order of Redemption is born again, lives and dies to live in Christ. This life is incomplete without death; and the visible church building is incomplete in its witness to this world without this outreach to the dead.

The churchyard belongs to the whole community represented by a parish, and not simply to the smaller group of parishioners who worship regularly in the church. The present generation will be judged by the way it cares for the resting place of its departed members. Grass is the usual covering of the ground. Economic considerations have diminished the enthusiasm of those who would have had the whole area a lawn and there has been a commendable return to the ancient method of keeping the grass short by grazing. Gravestones are not simply to be regarded as obstacles, preventing the speedy manoeuvre of the lawnmower; they are markers indicating the burial places of bodies beneath, and records in stone of the history of the parish.

Ecologically there are many churchyards which are natural conservation areas. The subtlety of their constituents means that great sensitivity is needed to maintain a balance between complete chaos on the one hand and obsessive tidiness on the other. But these positive principles imply corresponding negative assertions.

First, the churchyard is not the same as an area around a house; nor is it simply a curtilage, nor solely a garden. It is the area around a *church*. There is no necessity for exotic garden flowers, flower beds for annuals, or herbaceous borders. How many of these are generously donated, care lavished on them for a short period of time, and then neglected! Rarely does enthusiasm last until the time when the roses grow old and need replacement. Most herbaceous plants need to be dug up annually; again, too many small shrubs or flowering cherries can soon transform a churchyard into the resemblance of a suburban garden. The time-honoured name is 'God's Acre', which presents the sturdy image of a good agricultural field with solid forest trees on the boundary. Sir John Betjeman has expressed all that is intended here in succinct and memorable words:

> I hate to see in old churchyards
> Tombstones stacked round like playing cards
> Along the wall which then encloses
> A trim new lawn and standard roses,
> Bird-baths and objects such as fill a
> Garden in some suburban villa.
> The Bishop comes; the bird-bath's blessed.
> Our churchyard's now a 'garden of rest'
> And so it may be; all the same
> Graveyard's a much more honest name.
> *Poems in the Porch*, SPCK, 1954

Perhaps the most powerful pressure on churchyards has come from those who would have this area excessively neat and tidy (see Fig 1). Many look askance at the churchyard and criticise its long grass and unkempt appearance. There are some villages where not a single blade of grass at roadside or in garden may grow more than an inch! The cult of the lawn can lead its devotees to the point where all gravestones have to be sacrificed in honour of the omnivorous mower. To keep the churchyard looking like a lawn is expensive in equipment and labour and, we would argue, ecologically inappropriate. While we grant that in certain circumstances there may be a case for the close cutting of grass, we repeat our primary contention that the intrinsic character of a churchyard as 'the area round a church where the dead are buried' should be preserved. However, a compromise is needed between an excuse for complete neglect and obsessive tidiness, and we commend the simple expedient of cutting the grass short beside paths and leaving the rest for occasional cutting (see Chapter 14). This treatment keeps the proper character of the churchyard at minimal expense.

Secondly, a churchyard is not simply a setting for an ancient monument. At the centre of a churchyard stands not a ruin or a museum but a church, a place of worship for some day by day or week by week, for others, who attend the house of God less frequently, for baptisms, weddings and funerals. Even those churches which are vested in the Redundant Churches Fund (approximately two hundred and twenty of them) are still consecrated buildings, still 'holy places'; and their churchyards have not lost their theological significance. Much as one may admire the smooth lawns around an ancient abbey or castle whose grounds are kept up by English Heritage, there is no necessity for the churchyard's sward to be so closely clipped. To maintain such a high standard costs money and most parishes cannot, indeed ought not to, expend large sums in this way. A fee is paid for entry to most ancient monuments; there is no such fee for a parish church.

Thirdly, a churchyard is not simply a place where the dead are buried. That could be a definition of any burial ground or public cemetery. While it is true that many cemeteries have a chapel or building as a central feature, these have relevance only to the dead. A church, as we have already stated, is concerned equally with the living. There is a geographical aspect too. A cemetery may serve a very wide area. Many are vast in scale. The churchyard, on the other hand, is the burial ground of a particular group of people – those who live in its parish. It is often possible to find groups of gravestones commemorating several generations of the same family. As an old law-case has it, churchyards are where parishioners

> become entitled by law . . . to render back their remains into the earth, the common mother of mankind, without payment for the ground which they were to occupy.

Whereas in a public cemetery there was little attempt until the introduction of 'lawn cemeteries' to promote any congruity between adjacent headstones, in the churchyard a self-discipline of restraint has been exercised over the years to create some harmony of effect. While public cemeteries date for the most part from the nineteenth century, many a churchyard contains burials from the foundation of the church in the Middle Ages or earlier. Again, under recent legislation, permission for a memorial stone to stand in a cemetery is given only for a specified number of years; in a churchyard there is no such period defined, though some diocesan Chancellors are moving towards licences for a minimum fixed term.

An integral part of the churchyard's character lies in the gravestones. They ought not to be removed to stand around the wall, where they are separated from the remains whose position is recorded. These stones tell the history of a parish perhaps for 300 years or more; they reflect what people feel about death and bereavement and what craftsmen feel about design and expression – and how taste in these matters constantly changes. The inscriptions not only record names, but details of relationships and occupations recorded nowhere else. There are the simple late seventeenth- or early eighteenth-century stones of local material and craftsmanship (see Fig 2); those of neo-classical elegance (see Fig 3); then the Victorian ones which reveal a great variety in the letter-cutter's art (see Fig 4). It is also not uncommon for a headstone to record some tragic event, like that at Thursley in Surrey (see Fig 5) which commemorates a sailor who was 'barbarously murdered'. Recent years have seen an increase in interest in these stones as historical records. As our contemporary society endeavours to find its roots, so it goes also to every historical artefact to discover something about its ancestors. Family-history societies and groups grow at an increasing pace and help to lead the field in transcribing the inscriptions on tombstones, which may otherwise be obliterated by age or atmospheric pollution. However, the over-zealous cleaning of stones to discover and read the wording presents its own problems of aesthetics and conservation. The removal of lichen may expose the words but leave an abraded area subject to more rapid decay and, at the same time, destroy the lichenological evidence.

Archaeologists have in recent years produced valuable accounts of churchyards, e.g. at Cannington in Somerset, at Wharram Percy and St Helen on the Walls, York, Barton-on-Humber in Humberside and Deerhurst in Gloucestershire, to name but a few. There is much, however, still to learn and to interpret about the morphology and historical development of churchyards. It is well known that the north side was considered in medieval times as the place for burial of the suicide and unbaptised and this accounts partly for the absence of earlier stones in this area; in fact many churches were originally built up close to a northern boundary.

The churchyard and its stones are part of the English scene. The stones provide the scale by which to measure the church. Remove them and, if there are no trees, there may be nothing to which the church can be visually related. It is not without good reason that the photographer of a landscape includes some object in the foreground, a person or a tree for example, to provide his picture with the necessary scale. In this he follows the painter and the engraver.

The past two centuries have seen considerable changes in agricultural practice. Of all the grassland in the parish the churchyard's sward alone may have survived undisturbed, untouched perhaps for hundreds of years. With so many pasturelands and parklands being ploughed up or treated with herbicide and grass regulants, churchyards often contain the only surviving remnants of ancient undisturbed grassland (see Fig 6).

The most valuable areas have proved to be those which were enclosed in the nineteenth century but have not been buried in, and so preserve the oldest sward. Here grow wild flowers in profusion; and they should be encouraged to grow. The wildness of a country churchyard can sometimes be peculiarly apt, and the stable environment a positive encouragement for a rich mixture of flora and fauna. In a Suffolk churchyard some years ago the County Naturalists' Trust was able to identify more than 300 different varieties of wild flowers and flowering grasses, including a rarely found orchid, and this can be paralleled in many other places where surveys have been carried out. As Gerard Manley Hopkins wrote in *Invershaid*:

What would the world be, once bereft
Of wet and wildness? Let them be left,
O let them be left, wildness and wet
Long live the weeds and the wilderness yet.

Some churchyards are the only places where wild orchids can be found; others shelter rare grasses and wild flowers. Long grass is the habitat of the vole and other small animals, which in turn provide the food for hawks and kestrels. The trees, alive and dead, provide nesting places for birds and the source of their food supply. The hedges are often the only ones that remain in the district and perform a similar function. Even the lichen is of special interest to the naturalist. Each dated tombstone records the birthday of the lichen colony. Moreover, many lichens are of singular beauty. A recent book, *God's Acre* (1985) by Francesca Greenoak, provides in a most attractive form a book which draws attention to the natural delights of the churchyard in terms of flora and fauna.

Amongst many factors affecting country churchyards in recent years has been the considerable decrease in the number of burials. The practice of cremation has had its impact upon the churchyard over the past hundred years. Cremations now account for well over sixty per cent. The Church has endeavoured to demonstrate its concern for the departed by allocating areas for the interment of cremated remains; but these have by no means been used as much as was expected, and visually they frequently leave a great deal to be desired. It is perhaps also doubtful whether the percentage of cremations will increase in country districts. Many people continue to prefer the traditional method of earth burial and like to have the opportunity of erecting a suitable memorial over the place where the dead are interred, so that they can pay their respects as part of the 'work of mourning'. In our crowded island, however, other ways of providing for the 'work of mourning' have to be explored with both sensitivity and imagination. Complaints have reached us that the use of a 'Book of Remembrance' is experienced as an inadequate substitute, but how often is this option really followed through? It is not enough simply to provide such a Book and for the inscription of names and dates. It must be a beautiful object in its own right and be

9

placed in a suitable setting, there must be access to it by the bereaved, and there should be provision for flowers and candles, especially at the Year's Mind or anniversary of the death.

In the previous edition we gave some encouragement to parishes to satisfy this yearning by the laying of a small stone slab. In retrospect we recognise that this was a fundamental mistake – some churchyards are fast being covered with crazy paving. We urge therefore that serious consideration be given to alternative forms of commemoration, for instance alongside paths, as suggested in the chapter on 'Disposal after Cremation,' or by the provision of well-designed group memorials. There is also a very considerable opportunity for good design here, and parishes would be well advised to consult their architect, or a specialist landscape architect or garden designer, about the design and layout of areas for the interment of cremated remains.

The development of modern technology has had further repercussions on the monument industry. The Council for the Care of Churches continues to do all within its power to encourage the true craftsman. But, sadly, the development of machinery has enabled the production of large numbers of similar stones cheaply. These can be supplied ready-made with only the inscription to be added. The disappearance of the local stone-mason has led to the increase of mail-order firms who advertise nationally but whose wares are more suitable for the cemetery than the churchyard. Choice of a gravestone demands not only knowledge of the local regulations but a sensitivity in judging the right stone and design for a particular churchyard. In the past few years the practice of undertakers advising on the design of the gravestone as part of the 'package' has increased. This is highly commendable when the undertaker works in conjunction with the local sculptor or stonemason, but it is highly inappropriate, in our view, that pressure about the style or form of a memorial should be brought at so early a stage on people in the process of grieving.

Many writers on churchyards have deplored the use of marble, and particularly white marble. In retrospect it was perhaps as much the shapes that were constructed from this material as the material itself which caused such offence. Experience has shown that some white marbles lose their shiny surface and become covered with lichens as the years pass. Nevertheless we recommend strongly against the use of marble, since this material, especially with any degree of polish, is wholly unsympathetic to the traditional character of the English churchyard and white marble in particular will generally strike the observer as a 'sore thumb'.

We commented in 1976 upon the possible misuse of black polished granite with glaring gold letters. Since then there have been further developments in the use of this material, with stones incorporating engravings and vignettes of a character quite novel to the English churchyard. Some have even urged that the alien nature of this stone should cause it to be banned altogether. We would only urge, however, that the introduction of this stone should be done with the greatest circumspection.

Plastic memorials have been subjected to practical and scientific tests and have also been found unsatisfactory on a still greater number of counts. They are easily scratched or burnt, and readily dissolved by common chemicals. They are therefore not to be contemplated for use in English churchyards.

It is surely right to state as a principle that in a churchyard, as in a church, natural or sympathetic materials will always look best, and should always be preferred to the synthetic. The illustrations in this new edition endeavour to show the approach of a new generation to the design of churchyard memorials, and make clear that there is no need to follow exclusively Georgian or classical models in order to produce something of distinction. It should be recognised that, in order to stay in business, the memorial industry has had to become highly mechanised. This, however, need not preclude the production of good designs.

The churchyard should be the responsibility of the community and as many people as possible involved in its care and upkeep. The parish of Penn in Buckinghamshire does this excellently through a Churchyard Guild. Some parishes maintain a Churchyard Fund; some have established bodies of Friends, parallel to those established for many church buildings, who raise money for and assume responsibility for the regular maintenance and upkeep of the churchyard; others have a special Gift Day once a year. Bequests and donations may be invited not only from regular church members but from parishioners in general. It should, however, be made clear that such gifts are intended for the upkeep of the churchyard as a whole and cannot be earmarked for a particular grave. Parishes have sometimes found themselves committed to maintaining a particular memorial in return for a donation which, though reasonable enough at the time it was given, has been rendered wholly inadequate by inflation.

A churchyard is like a work of art, and any scheme for altering or improving it should be soundly based on conservation principles and only put in hand after taking knowledgeable advice on the different aspects involved, and after proper authorization has been received. In any instance where it is proposed to do more than deal with grass, flowers and shrubs, it is necessary that the Diocesan Advisory Committee for the Care of Churches should be consulted, and a faculty obtained. The rights of all parishioners are involved and people are naturally very sensitive on the question of graves.

It is strongly recommended that parochial church councils protect themselves from difficulties, and also give the bereaved positive guidance and advice, by adopting rules for the control and management of their churchyard. These rules should also make crystal clear what procedures should be followed for the introduction of new memorials into the churchyard. They must explain the nature of the Chancellor's jurisdiction, and express succinctly what sizes, forms, and materials are allowed at the Chancellor's discretion and may be agreed by the incumbent (or, in an interregnum, by the Rural Dean). Our new suggested rules are intended as a model for this purpose, both at diocesan and at parochial level. It cannot be emphasised too strongly that, while meeting a legitimate need for guidance, the adoption and wider local promulgation of such regulations will protect the incumbent and the parochial church council from any suggestion of arbitrariness or bias. The adoption of such rules also enables a clear break to be made between earlier, and maybe unsatisfactory, policies and fresh and more positive guidelines for the future. Anything out of the ordinary run of memorials can still be submitted to the Chancellor, via the Registrar, for authorization by faculty if the Chancellor considers that a sufficient case has been made for an exception. Artistic quality should always be preferred to the mundane and stereotyped.

Where a churchyard is vested in the Redundant Churches Fund the incumbent, churchwardens and parochial church council cease to have any rights or responsibilities. Neither does the faculty jurisdiction apply. Burials may take place only if the Fund specifically gives permission, and this is only in special cases. Most of the churchyards owned by the Fund have been so vested because of their historic interest and in order to safeguard the aesthetic impact of the church. Consequently, proposed memorials are subject to strict scrutiny and in some cases are not permitted.

We recommend that parishes should not only conserve what is best in the historical development of the churchyard, but plan wisely for future development. It may well be that, when a new section of the churchyard is opened, there should be a stricter design code about the type of memorial stone. This is especially important when a churchyard is re-used after a period of disuse, and new stones will be erected near others which have been in existence for a century or more. Indeed, such an opportunity will enable a parish to consider a consistent policy from the start, embracing the planting of trees and shrubs, erecting walls or fences, and the layout of paths, as well as laying down guidelines for the monuments. As urged before, proper professional advice, e.g. from a landscape architect, will be likely to secure a better result than a 'do it yourself' or laissez-faire approach.

The care of the churchyard embraces many of the factors which most closely touch our present generation – a concern for conservation, both of wild life and of our artistic and architectural heritage; a concern for visual values, and for good design; a need for solitude and beauty, away from the pressures and difficulties of life; a desire for significance, and a resolution of the interdependent mysteries of life and death. To be responsible for a churchyard, large or small, should be seen as an opportunity and a privilege, and as a way of relating to the wider community. In this Handbook we try, as far as we can, to provide practical and clearly understandable advice which will make this task lighter, and also richly rewarding.

2

The History of the Churchyard

Although burials associated with first pagan and then Christian sacred sites and buildings have been taking place for thousands of years, the appearance of the churchyard as we know it is largely a post-Reformation product. Saxon and later medieval monuments do survive, more frequently than is often realised, but often buried or unregarded; sometimes thay will have been relocated inside the church, or (if of particular artistic interest) deposited in a museum. Many of the sepulchral slabs to be seen in churches were originally in the churchyard, with small stones set at the head and foot of the slab. Some can still be found in churchyards and should be carefully preserved. A particularly fine medieval monument surviving in an English churchyard is the fourteenth-century tomb at Loversall, near Doncaster; the fine tomb-chest outside the east of the chancel of Muchelney in Somerset dates from the fifteenth century. Sixteenth-century headstones are usually very small and can easily be overlooked.

The development of churchyard monuments in the seventeenth and eighteenth centuries is due to a considerable degree to the rise of a prosperous middle class of merchants, landowners, farmers and skilled craftsmen. The demand for churchyard monuments spread gradually down the social scale, while the interiors of churches continued to receive the memorials of the most wealthy and influential families until well into the present century. The oft-quoted epitaph written by an eighteenth-century wit for his own monument at Kingsbridge, Devon, sums it up rather neatly:

> Here lie I at the Chancel door
> Here lie I because I'm poor
> The further in the more you'll pay
> Here lie I as warm as they.

The social implications of the churchyard are significant in a variety of ways. A churchyard often provides a fascinating record of English life over more than three centuries. The mere presence of a monument, however decayed, and however illegible its inscription, can be of great value to the local historian. Monuments can be dated with reasonable accuracy without recourse to inscriptions and they thus give a clue to the size and relative prosperity of a community at any given time. Local variations abound and, in almost every case, they provide visual evidence of local life which is available from no other source. Above all the churchyard was, and ought still to be, a vivid symbol of the church's care and concern for its parishioners not only in this life but also in that beyond the grave. Within the churchyard there was ample visual evidence that the dead had been finally 'gathered in' and the tombstone was not only a marker for the body but a statement of faith in the resurrection and the glorious life hereafter. It was this attitude which dictated the use of symbolism in tombstone design and it was this aspect of the churchyard which made the nonconformists so adamant about burial within their own graveyards. In symbolic terms, therefore, the clearance of a graveyard has implications which require the fullest and most heartsearching consideration before any drastic and irreversible action is taken.

The sudden rise of the churchyard monument during the seventeenth century is in itself a matter of considerable interest. The Council for the Care of Churches would be glad to know of churchyard monuments, especially those previously unrecorded, dating from before 1700, so that a central record may be kept. All such information will also be passed on to the Royal Commission on Historical Monuments. It must be remembered that, throughout the seventeenth and much of the following century, the transport of stone over any but the shortest distance was so difficult and expensive as to be almost unthinkable for such purposes as graveyard monuments. It was not until the canals, and later the railways, began to make bulk transport of materials a possibility that varieties of stone appeared in graveyards. Before the building of the canals, village communities were largely self-supporting and the stone for memorials, like that for building, would come from local quarries. The men who carved them would be local craftsmen who, certainly until the late eighteenth century, and in many cases up until more recent times, would spend much of their lives working on the repair and construction of vernacular buildings. It seems likely that they built up a stock of gravestones in the winter months when other work was scarce, and then added the inscriptions later, as and when they were required. Their skills, together with many of the designs, were handed down from one generation to another – often within the same family. When outside influences affected the life of the community, these are frequently reflected in sudden changes in tombstone design. Particularly fine examples of this can be seen in many Gloucestershire churchyards, where the charming rusticity of earlier stones was superseded by sophisticated designs of great beauty during the period when architects and masons of the highest ability were engaged in supplying the local gentry with elegant houses in landscaped parks. The influence of theories about the nature of landscape and the picturesque were so powerful that some who could well afford otherwise preferred an outdoor setting for their monuments. An excellent example is the mausoleum in the churchyard at Hambleden, Buckinghamshire, seen against the background of a park-like setting.

Not only does the churchyard display the rapid change from rusticity to sophistication in the leaders of rural society during the eighteenth century, it also reflects the spread of wealth during the same period. The influence of the 'Age of Elegance' is scarcely better displayed than it is in some English churchyards – especially when seen in a total relationship embracing great house, park, church and village. Many of the best examples of eighteenth-century design and craftsmanship can be found in what are even now remote graveyards in the deep countryside.

Earlier lettering – often delightful, but crude – was generally replaced in the eighteenth century by skilled versions of the Roman alphabet or virtuoso interpretations of pen or engraved forms. In the Midlands, the carvers of slate tombstones from the Swithland quarries were signing their work as 'engravers', and the specialised craftsman mason was beginning to appear.

The second great period of churchyard memorials began with

the advent of the nineteenth century. For at least the first half of the century tombstones are an invaluable source of information on local history at a time of great unheaval and social change. Midland slates travelled up the newly-opened navigations, and their inscriptions plot the dates of canal openings with accuracy. Cast-iron memorials from the Coalbrookdale foundry (the 'birthplace' of the Industrial Revolution) spread into the Shropshire churchyards as a very acceptable substitute for local stone of mediocre quality. Thus, a rusted iron monument with no legible inscription can have importance in terms of local history as well as being one of those visual details which give character to the local scene.

By the beginning of the second quarter of the nineteenth century the production of monuments had reached a peak in quantity with little diminution of quality. The old standards of genteel lettering had been replaced by a robust use of every available letter form, with a sense of design allied to craftsmanship which has not since been equalled. Never before or since has cut lettering been put to better or more varied use than on the tombstones (particularly the slates) of the early years of the last century. Similarly, the old symbols were being replaced by a more varied range which was only later subdued, first by the exponents of Gothic and later by the more fertile sentimental imagery of the late Victorians. In dealing with these, it is as well to remember that fashions change and that what we may dislike our children may well admire. Churchyards reveal changes in taste and fashion over the years and there is a danger of obliterating the evidence of a period whose attitudes and imagery do not happen to be in accord with our own. A considerable degree of humility is required of us when advising what stones, if any, should be permitted to be removed.

By the middle of the last century the pattern-book monuments had appeared. These stemmed from several sources, the combined effect of which caused the demise of local style in monuments and the initiative of local craftsmen. One was the book of 'suitable' designs, usually by respectable architects, which depicted the monuments based upon medieval tombs; another the publication of tracts by the clergy, vigorously propounding standards of ecclesiastical taste and propriety. Examples are *A Tract Upon Tombstones* by the Rev. Francis Paget (1843), *A Paper on Monuments* by the Rev. John Armstrong (1844), and *A Manual of Sepulchral Memorials* by the Rev. Edward Trollope, FSA, with a dedication to and a commendation by the Archbishop of Canterbury. A third was the catalogue of the newly emerged trade of monumental mason. This introduced new designs and new materials, neither of which had anything to do with the locality in which the monuments were to be erected. Thus began a trend which still continues today, and which has extended to include monuments of unsuitable foreign material, cut by foreign masons in foreign workshops, entirely divorced from our native traditions. Most of these are meaningless in almost every sense and they have done much to destroy the character of a large number of churchyards. It is a particular tragedy that they are frequently left in position when older memorials are removed in misguided attempts to 'tidy up'.

Towards the end of the last century, the followers of William Morris and protagonists of the Arts and Crafts movement did a great deal to balance damage done by the commercialised production of monuments. It has been the flood of ready-made imported materials in the present century which has seemed virtually to stifle the vernacular tradition. In the years between the wars valiant attempts were made, notably by Eric Gill and Gilbert Ledward and their associates and followers, to raise standards and re-introduce native stones. Unfortunately these had insufficient effect on the overall picture and their works have an intellectual appeal which, though distinguished, was bound to be limited in its impact. What is needed today is the total rejection of mass-produced gravestones, a willingness to allow original designs, and positive encouragement for the use of appropriate (preferably local) materials or materials which closely correspond to indigenous stones.

In present conditions a monument is likely to last just as long as someone is prepared to look after it and it may be as well to encourage the use of wood – oak for preference, e.g. in the form of a single cross or graveboard. A really excellent example is illustrated from the churchyard at Busbridge, in Surrey; this oak gravemarker, weathered to a beautiful silvery-grey tonality, was erected in the 1930s to a young airman, and is still in good condition. It is also an example of the best-informed taste of its time and, happily enough, stands next to the group of stones of various members of the family of Gertrude Jekyll designed by their architect friend Sir Edwin Lutyens.

It cannot be too often stressed that monuments need not be elaborate to be good. It is not just cost which has excluded local craftsmen and materials, but a combination of widespread misunderstanding of the place and purpose of a monument, and the influence of salesmanship at a time of stress. Sound advice could often avert some of the horrors of contemporary graveyard design as well as ensuring fewer aesthetic or practical problems in the future. The nature of such advice is developed further in the chapter on Commissioning a New Memorial.

3

The Archaeological Value of Churchyards

Most medieval parish churchyards were in existence by the end of the eleventh century, and of these the majority are likely to be older. Just how ancient they may be is something that archaeologists are now trying to establish in a systematic way. But in northern England, in Lincolnshire, and parts of the north Midlands it is already clear from the presence of carved gravestones of pre-Conquest date that the history of a graveyard commonly reaches back to the tenth century. Some parish churches, especially those which originated as minsters, possess graveyards that are older still. And in south-west England and the west Midlands it is likely that there are churchyards which have their origins in enclosures established during the earliest years of British Christianity.

A point that arises from the antiquity of churchyards is that many different activities have taken place within them. Apart from burial itself, and early rites associated with it, the first church on the site is not necessarily to be expected beneath the present building, but may lie elsewhere within the enclosure, as was discovered at Rivenhall, Essex. Priests sometimes resided within the churchyard, as at Asheldham, Essex, where excavation revealed the remains of such a house; or Edenham, Lincolnshire, where the present rectory stands close to the church and may reflect a more ancient arrangement. Remains of former portions of the present church, like transepts, towers, or aisles, removed in the past, may await discovery. In some areas there was a tradition of free-standing towers, and the foundations of these may also lie beneath the turf. Pits for the casting of bells or the mixing of mortar may occur near the church; the archaeo-logical study of such features can assist understanding of the architectural development of the building. Churchyards were sometimes used for trading, and commercial activity may have left its traces in deposits of pottery or lost coins. In times of stress the churchyard was a useful place in which to hide coins or valuables. Such hoards have been encountered during grave-digging, as at Goldsborough, North Yorkshire, or quite recently at Pentney, Norfolk.

Another reason why churchyards are archaeologically impor-tant lies in the fact that items ejected from the church were commonly left in the churchyard, to be forgotten and eventually overgrown or buried. Examples include medieval fonts, items of statuary (e.g. following episodes of iconoclasm in the sixteenth and seventeenth centuries), architectural sculpture, and more fragmentary materials such as ancient window glass. Even things outcast in recent centuries (like, say, the mechanism of an eighteenth-century clock, or an old barrel organ) may now be of the greatest interest.

The primary function of the churchyard was, and usually still is, that of burial. Below ground this will be reflected in the presence of, usually, thousands of graves, often much intercut. If groundworks are necessary, it is well to remember that medieval graves were sometimes quite shallow, and that human remains can occur within a few inches of the modern ground surface. Churchyards have often changed shape, on occasion expanding in one direction while contracting in another. This means that a modern extension may encroach upon an area of the cemetery that was in use many centuries ago.

Repairs and gravedigging over the years have often turned up coffins and gravecovers of pre-Reformation date. Above ground the history of burial is therefore likely to be reflected in the presence of medieval sarcophagi (occasionally Roman ones, re-used), often placed *ex situ* near the church. Medieval and, in some areas, Anglo-Saxon gravestones of different kinds also com-monly survive, though they may be in fragmentary condition and are not always recognized for what they are. Occasionally coped medieval gravecovers have been used to cap the churchyard wall, as at Skipwith, Humberside, or Asgarby, Lincolnshire. Today this is not a practice to be recommended, for it will accelerate the decay of the stones.

One should always reflect upon what the site of the churchyard was used for before it was assigned to Christian purposes. Not infrequently there are signs of pre-Christian activity, such as prehistoric flints (e.g. Sanderstead, Surrey), domestic pottery of prehistoric, Roman or Anglo-Saxon date, hand-querns for the grinding of corn (e.g. High Hoyland, South Yorkshire), or even substantial Roman buildings, as at Woodchester, Gloucestershire, or Widford, Worcestershire. The takeover by Christians of sites of heathen worship, commonly assumed, is not in fact well represented in archaeological terms, although instances of depaganization may have occurred. The lofty prehistoric monolith in the churchyard at Rudston, Humberside, is a possible case in point.

All these different kinds of evidence need to be cared for. They are part of the history of the church and of the community which has used it. Looking after the archaeology of your churchyard is not onerous, provided that a few simple ground-rules are understood and followed.

The basic point to be grasped is that all archaeological evidence is in a state of decay. Decay is inevitable and cannot be halted. It can, however, be slowed down, and the aim should therefore be to identify policies of management which will ensure that the rate of decay is kept as low as possible.

Translated into practice this means avoiding, where practicable, actions that would disturb buried deposits; or thinking hard about a place for the keeping of carved stones which will give them maximum protection. It also means reporting new discoveries (e.g. of sculpture, a coin hoard, pottery, flints) that may be made in the course of gravedigging or minor groundworks. Such reporting is desirable for two reasons: first, so that advice can be given on any steps that may be needed to conserve what has been found; and second, so that the nature and location of the discovery can be added to the county Sites and Monuments Record (SMR). Looked upon individually such finds may seem trivial, but when mapped in company with others elsewhere, patterns emerge which can assist in the writing of better history.

If an object of gold or silver is discovered this must be reported to the police, as the coroner may decide to make it the subject of a treasure trove inquest.

Where extensive changes are contemplated within or beside the churchyard (e.g. the re-routing of a boundary, a churchyard extension, a new building, or a car park) it is always necessary to take archaeological advice. This is easily done, because every diocese should have appointed its own archaeological consultant. The address or telephone number of your diocesan archaeological consultant may be obtained from the DAC Secretary, or from the CCC.

Usually such consultation will lead simply to an 'all clear', or to a request that an archaeologist be posted to observe some of the works. Just occasionally there will be a request from the consultant that the site be examined scientifically before the new works take place. In cases of this sort the consultant will put the parish in touch with an organization that can do the work properly (e.g. a county archaeological unit, a university department, or a competent local society). If such work then takes place it is normally funded from an external source, such as the Historic Buildings and Monuments Commission (English Heritage), the local authority, or museum. There is a CCC booklet entitled *Churches and Archaeology,* which explains about this in more detail.

The essential point to remember about consulting the diocesan archaeologist is to *consult early.* Never put it off until the last minute, for at this stage it may be too late for the archaeologist to arrange for appropriate coverage, or to suggest an adjustment to the scheme which could have left the evidence undisturbed. Do not imagine that archaeologists are eager to dig up your churchyard: conservation and preservation of evidence are nearly always preferred to investigation. So if any sort of action, even a 'watching brief', is called for, the further ahead it can be planned for the better it will be for both parties – and of course for the archaeological evidence that is so often latent in a churchyard, and of which the parish is usually, and justifiably proud.

Guidance on the keeping and display of worked stones is now

available in a booklet published by the CCC. A more detailed manual is published by the Council for British Archaeology (112 Kennington Road, London SE11 6RE; tel 01-582 0494).

The Council for British Archaeology takes a close interest in all matters to do with the archaeological study of churches, and can be relied upon to give advice on academic matters, either directly, or by putting the parish in touch with a suitable scholar. (You may like to bear this in mind in connection not only with churchyard management, but other things such as anniversary festivals, lectures, or the preparation of a guide-book). The CBA also keeps lists of the diocesan consultants, and of professional archaeological bodies and local societies. If in doubt, ring them: they are accustomed to receiving such inquiries and will always be glad to help you.

4

Churchyard Monuments and Other Features

Mention was made in a previous chapter of medieval churchyard monuments. Where these survive they should be allowed to remain *in situ* unless they require the protection of being brought indoors. Medieval churchyard monuments should not be confused with monuments, perhaps just as ancient, removed from inside the church by Victorian or earlier restorers, but never designed for an outdoor site. In many cases these should be brought under cover again. All medieval monuments, whatever their condition, should be carefully preserved, though it may well be that their condition will dictate where they are to be preserved. Advice on their preservation may be sought through the Diocesan Advisory Committee or the Conservation Officer of the Council for the Care of Churches.

In an average churchyard of some antiquity, the earliest monuments will probably date from the latter part of the seventeenth century, and earlier ones will be uncommon. A really fine late-sixteenth-century example is illustrated, now brought inside the church of Windrush in Gloucestershire. Seventeenth-century and earlier tombstones can at times be quite crude in execution; some even have a 'home-made' quality which adds to, rather than detracts from, their charm. Most older monuments, however, are of the eighteenth century. To this period belong most of the baroque, rococo or neo-classical box or chest-tombs, among which is a great variety of weathered texture and craftsmanship of rare beauty. In some localities, a profusion of delicately carved headstones also remains from this period.

REGIONAL FEATURES

All over the country it is possible to trace characteristics of the local stonemasons who worked in the district. Much of their work shows originality and freshness combined with great refinement of execution. There are the typical groups of memorials of the Cotswolds and the adjacent counties (where good stone was abundant) and of Warwickshire, Leicestershire and Derbyshire, as well as of Devon and Cornwall, where the masons produced an astonishing development of fine lettering and ornament on slabs of slate. Even the more commonplace late-eighteenth- and early-nineteenth-century memorials carved in Portland and other stones are very worthy of preservation, as showing what could be done with moderate means and good material.

Many factors are involved in the decline of quality of memorials produced in the nineteenth century. Some good examples continued to be produced, but generally both the quality of the stone and the skill with which it was cut degenerated. The fine stone box-tombs developed into brick boxes rendered to look like stone, though some interesting examples were made of cast iron, as at Burford, in Oxfordshire, and sometimes in other counties where iron-founding was carried out. Headstones lost their ornaments; lettering of good design lingered on, but with the passage of the nineteenth century it began to lose character. Throughout the first quarter of the nineteenth century fine indoor work was being done by famous sculptors such as Chantrey, Flaxman, Westmacott and many lesser-known, yet the great English tradition dies down, slowly but surely, to a period of unimaginative dullness, to be succeeded by a flood of feeble, pretentious productions which has regrettably increased until our own day.

DUTY TO PRESERVE

It is clear, therefore, that virtually all earlier churchyard monuments are worthy of careful preservation, because of their originality of design and skill of craftsmanship. They must be seen as part of the cultural heritage for which the Church accepts a custodian's responsibility. Although they remain technically in private ownership, the family concerned may have died out; their maintenance falls within the general upkeep of the churchyard.

Iron railings round graves were chiefly needed for protection from thieves, gamblers, drunkards, body-snatchers, sheep and cows, or to prevent the desecration of graves of unpopular parishioners in a rougher age. Many railings have been destroyed. Some of those remaining from the eighteenth and nineteenth centuries are now valuable because rare and should be retained and kept painted. Railings may also be listed as being of special architectural or historical interest, or as forming part of the setting of a listed monument. On the other hand, where railings enclose areas abutting on the church, and prevent needed access to walls, windows, damp corners and rain pipes, their removal may prove necessary. Railings should not be allowed to become too entangled with ivy and briars.

When plain brick chest-tombs break up, the sides can be removed and the top slab placed upon the foundation of the tomb. However, where this is done the flat stones may eventually sink, and the grass grow over them. Sunken or crooked headstones can be reset vertically, the hole being filled with rubble well tamped down to give a firm foundation beneath the turf. Ruthless straightening is neither desirable nor necessary.

REMOVAL OF GRAVESTONES

Where overcrowding makes grass-cutting difficult, application for a faculty may be sought for the removal of gravestones and for a few carefully selected stones to be reset in some other, less crowded, part of the churchyard. This would also perhaps provide an opportunity for removing a really fine headstone into the church porch, for protection. If a stone is moved indoors for protection, its original position should be made clear on a plan indicating position, orientation and size. No headstone should be removed without due consideration to its value in its natural setting. Care should be taken not to disrupt groups of family graves. A trench cut round such a group may well solve a problem here, and also serve to emphasise the family group.

Serried ranks of stones round the boundaries look ugly and collect more weeds and brambles. Stones should *never* be collected against the wall of the church itself because moisture will then become trapped between them causing decay in both the church walls and the headstones.

In Cheshire and Lancashire and parts of Yorkshire it has long been traditional to provide a thick tombstone lying flat on the ground, so that eventually the whole churchyard will be paved over. In these districts the tradition should be maintained if practicable, as the stone used was hard and enduring. This is very different, however, from the practice of laying flat a quantity of thin headstones in a district where they were made to stand upright. Aesthetically this is not desirable, and such treatment leads to their decay.

In Kent and elsewhere in the south-east of England, from late in the eighteenth century onwards, it was sometimes the custom to place an uninscribed stone between the head and footstone to protect the gravespace. These took many forms, sometimes consisting of a flat narrow piece of stone, or a semi-cylindrical or coped stone. Others look like stone coffins and in (but not peculiar to) the Home Counties, the stone was shaped in such a way as to resemble a mummified body. These 'body-stones' are of historical value and they should certainly not be removed or destroyed. However, they do present difficulties in churchyard maintenance and as the majority of churchyards will only possess a few, the simplest solution is to cut a trench round the whole grave. The smaller stones sometimes found at the foot of graves ought to be retained *in situ* as much as headstones. If it is absolutely essential to move a footstone for maintenance reasons, it should be placed at the back of the headstone and not against the inscription. It should never be moved away from the grave and placed elsewhere in the churchyard.

GENERAL MAINTENANCE

As a general rule, lettering on gravestones should not be re-cut, though it may be repainted. Cleaning is preferable, and this requires some expert knowledge, since the treatment required will vary according to the nature of the stone.

Where it is desired to remove lichen or green mould from churchyard monuments, detergents, soda, or soap preparations containing it should not be used for washing stone. It is most important first to ascertain the condition of the stone surface. If this is in any way unsound, then expert advice should be sought before any cleaning is attempted. Moss and lichen on recumbent stones may be easily removed, to make the inscription legible, by covering the stone with a light coating of earth for two or three weeks, and then brushing it off. On vertical stones in sound condition, the worst of the moss and lichen may be removed by the careful use of a blunt wooden scraper, followed by the application of a biocide, following closely the maker's instruction. After suitable time has elapsed the dead moss and lichen may be removed with a bristle brush. If a fractured stone or broken chest-tomb is to be repaired, non-ferrous metal dowels should be used, as iron rusts, expands and splits the stone in which it is bedded. Chest-tombs are seldom mortared together, but if mortar is needed to repair them, a soft lime mortar should be used. In all but the most straightforward cases, a competent stone conservator should be asked to advise, and frequently to carry out the work. Advice on suitable stone conservators may be obtained from the Conservation Officer of the Council for the Care of Churches.

In many parts of south-east England, where stone was scarce and timber plentiful, a wooden memorial was often erected, consisting of a framed board extending lengthwise over the grave attached to a small wooden post at each end bearing a painted inscription. These structures, known in some places as bed-heads and in others as leaping boards, were usually painted white and lettered in black; occasionally they were surrounded by an ornamental wooden cresting; sometimes the posts had decorative finials, and sometimes a row of iron spikes was placed along the top to prevent children sitting on the edge. Being of wood and usually on the graves of the less wealthy, these bed-heads have tended to decay. Falling to pieces as they generally do through the action of the weather, their remains have frequently been cleared away as rubbish. Wherever possible, any that remain should be repaired and retained as long as they will hold together. The inscriptions were usually painted, not carved, and there is no reason why they should not be repainted, if the style of the original letter is carefully copied. It is doubtful if any example remains earlier than the nineteenth century. A few were set up in remoter parishes as late as the last quarter of that century and there have been sporadic revivals of the custom up to the present day. It is probable that this attractive form of memorial represents a very ancient tradition, perhaps going back into the Middle Ages; it deserves to be encouraged and revived.

Much information about older churchyard monuments, together with good illustrations, will be found in books listed in the Bibliography. More detailed and specific advice on the conservation of churchyard monuments of artistic and historic interest may be obtained from the Council for the Care of Churches and from the Historic Buildings and Monuments Commission for England (English Heritage).

CHURCHYARD CROSSES

Ancient Crosses

The churchyard cross often preceded the erection of a church building. In very early Saxon times, when these buildings were scarcely distinguishable from secular ones, such a symbol was essential.

The cross was the predominant feature in every churchyard before the Reformation. In districts where good stone is abundant, medieval survivals – often fragmentary – are common. On either side of the Bristol Channel, and also in many parts of the Midlands, there is scarcely a churchyard which does not have some considerable fragments. Occasionally, as at Chewton Mendip and Stringston in Somerset, and at St Donats and Llangan in the Vale of Glamorgan, the cross is complete; so also are many of the earlier crosses in Cornwall. In eastern and south-eastern England, however, remains of churchyard crosses are exceptional. We know from documents that they existed, but they must often have been of wood and therefore easily destroyed by the Puritans or by the elements and, in later times, perhaps removed to make room for graves.

All remains of churchyard crosses should, of course, be faithfully recorded and preserved. It is long since any such relics were wilfully destroyed but there have been some injurious, although well intentioned, restorations of ancient crosses. Heads and shafts of purely conjectural, if not actually misleading, type have been added to old bases, and these have been too heavily repaired in order to support the new work. Here and there an original head has been recovered and replaced. This is generally the right course, but opportunities of doing it are not likely to occur very frequently. The fixing of a new head to an ancient shaft is not without practical as well as aesthetic risks, as the ancient stone may split on the insertion of dowels or, as a result of the increased weight, through wind resistance or leverage.

As a general rule, remains of churchyard crosses should be no more than cleaned and conserved, and not restored by the addition of new work. Even this treatment requires specialist advice. Where the steps are loose or sundered by vegetation they may need to be reset, care being taken to use the proper method of pointing. If they have sunk into the ground, they can be prised up and reset. Such an exercise may provide an opportunity for archaeological investigation and should never be attempted without the involvement of the diocesan archaeological consultant and the church architect.

Modern Crosses

Where remains of an old cross exist, and it is desired to erect a new one, an entirely different design should preferably be chosen. By ancient tradition the cross was generally near the principal entrance to the church. Where no traces of an old cross survive, the new one may be placed nearby but the cross should not be too near the building. Wherever it is placed, it should always face towards the west, like the rood or the altar cross within the church. The adoption of this common-sense rule, always observed of old, does much to secure an appearance of congruity with the church building.

Where remains of an old cross exist, the new one should be placed elsewhere. Indeed it may be preferable to set up the new cross in a dominating position as an extension of the churchyard. The churchyard extension at Penn in Buckinghamshire provides an excellent example of this. The late Sir Edwin Maufe, who designed the new extension, retained the eighteenth-century red brick former garden walls to give a sense of enclosure and placed his formal layout within the space so enclosed. Conspicuously placed at the junction of the main axes is the cross, carved by sculptor Darsie Rawlins, who lives locally. On one side is the Holy Spirit in the form of a dove, and on the other is carved the Blessed Virgin and the Holy Child – a choice of iconography which is both unusual and, in this context, moving.

Special care should be taken that a modern cross, especially if it is adjoining an ancient church, is neither too large nor too elaborate. The Diocesan Advisory Committee should always be consulted about the design and situation of a new cross or the repair of an old one.

OTHER STONES

In addition to the cross and gravestones, many churchyards contain such valuable antiquities as ancient sundials, parish stocks, and occasionally stone coffins, moulded or carved stones, monuments, or recumbent effigies which may at some time have been removed from the church.

Sundials on pedestals, usually dating from the eighteenth or early nineteenth century, are quite frequently found in church-yards in certain districts as, for example, in Cheshire. When excessively stained with algae, they may be cleaned, after taking proper advice. They may be in need of repair which will require sensitive handling. Treatment of their stone and iron-work is always a matter for specialist advice, either through the Diocesan Advisory Committee, the parish architect, or the Council for the Care of Churches.

Parish stocks still remain in quite a number of churchyards – they are frequently found in Cornwall, for example. Although their historical position in the churchyard is important, and

Plate 1. *Buckden, Cambridgeshire: large late gothic table-tomb.*

Plate 2. *Burford, Oxfordshire: early seventeenth-century Cotswold 'bale' tomb.*

Plate 3. *Burford, Oxfordshire: a group of headstones in 'rustic baroque' style.*

In Memory of
A generous, but unfortunate Sailor,
Who was barbaroufly murder'd on Hindhead,
On Sepr. 24th 1786.
By three Villains,
After he had liberally treated them,
And promifed them his farther Affiftance,
On the Road to Portfmouth.

When pitying Eyes to fee my Grave fhall come,
And with a generous Tear bedew my Tomb;
Here fhall they read my melancholy Fate,
With Murder and Barbarity complete.
In perfect Health, and in the Flow'r of Age,
I fell a Victim to three Ruffians Rage;
On bended Knees I mercy ftrove t' obtain,
Their Thirft of Blood made all Entreaties vain,
No dear Relation, or ftill dearer Friend,
Weeps my hard Lot, or miferable End;
Yet o'er my fad Remains, (my Name unknown,)

Plate 4. *Thursley, Surrey: a famous late eighteenth-century headstone telling a gruesome tale.*

Plate 5. *Thursley, Surrey: Greek Revival mausoleum-type monument.*

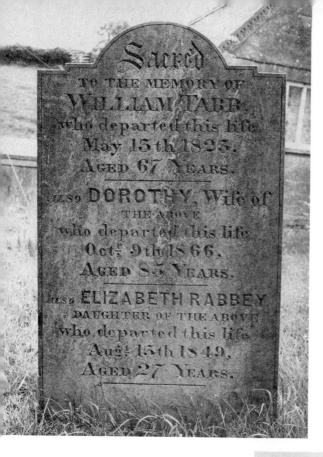

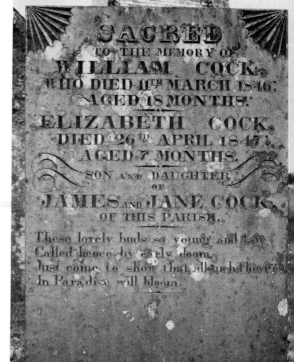

Plate 6a and 6b. *St Petroc Minor, Little Petherick, Cornwall: examples of exceptionally fine early-Victorian letter-cutting.*

Plate 7. *Cranleigh, Surrey: Norman Revival family vault, surrounded by excellent planting of good-sized trees.*

Plate 8. *Kimbolton, Cambridgeshire: a good example of a well-designed cross.*

Plate 9. *Burford, Oxfordshire: this fine tomb-chest of the 1860s is inspired by medieval exemplars.*

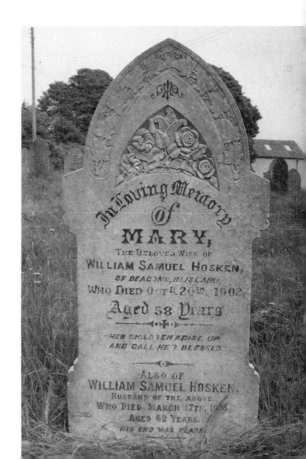

Plate 10. *St Protus and St Hyacinth, Blisland, Cornwall: the use of a pattern-book as here, need not necessarily lead to dullness.*

Plate 11.   *This headstone by Eric Gill in the cemetery at Compton, Surrey, shows the subtlety of his lettering and layout.*

should certainly be recorded if they are moved, it is often desirable for their preservation that they should be under cover. Sometimes a special shelter has been provided, or the porch has proved to be a suitable place. If necessary, they should be treated, when thoroughly dry, for beetle or dry rot. The iron parts can be painted, after first cleaning off all rust with wire wool, with a mixture of one part raw linseed oil to four parts turpentine, mixed with a few drops of terebene and coloured with Berlin black.

Medieval stone coffins are sometimes found lying in church-yards, where they may finally disintegrate through erosion caused by action of the weather. Wherever possible they should be placed under cover, together with any miscellaneous remains of ancient carved stonework, and it is an advantage if they can be labelled with a brief note to draw attention to their historical interest.

It is especially important to label the fragments of significant pre- and post-Conquest sculptured crosses and monuments found all over the north of England, in the north Midlands, in Cornwall and occasionally in other localities; and the medieval cross slabs and hogback stones which are more widely found but are, nevertheless, rare. Even the most fragmentary or unadorned pieces should be labelled and preserved, and careful watch kept for further finds which may turn up embedded in the church or churchyard walls, built into houses and farm buildings in the village, or even on the vicarage rockery. Often such fragments are all that remains of the earliest church or preaching centre in the village; and they may afford invaluable evidence for dating the foundation of the parish church.

If these stones are exhibited in the church great care should be taken in their arrangement, and expert advice (e.g. from the Area Museums Service) will need to be sought on identification and display. In some cases it may be preferable to record the stone and re-incorporate it in the church fabric. An aisle should not be a museum. In other cases, deposit in the local museum may be the appropriate solution.

It goes without saying that all such items and fragments should be listed in the Church Inventory.

A final word about below-ground evidence. Churchyards often contain the buried remains of earlier churches or ancient buildings, which may be encountered in almost any disturbance of the ground. New drainage trenches, the foundations of new walls or clearance for car parks in or near churchyards, are frequently the occasion for discovery of such remains, whose nature can only be established by an experienced archaeologist. The Council for British Archaeology has nominated a consultant for each diocese who will be pleased to advise. His name may be obtained from the Council or from the Secretary of the Diocesan Advisory Committee. It is essential that he should be consulted at the earliest possible stage in the discussions about any such proposal.

LYCH-GATES

The entrance to many churchyards is through some form of lych-gate. These gates are often thought of as ornamental archways, but in fact they take many forms, and are strictly functional in origin. Their purpose is to shelter the coffin and the bearers when a funeral procession pauses to await the priest coming out from the church to meet them.

In some places the centre of the gateway is occupied by a lych-stone, on which the body rested. In the western counties this may lie between two passage-ways or Cornish stiles with a seat on either side, but without any superstructure. Sometimes a wicket-gate may be provided at the side, for use when the central passage is not required, and there must be many places where the lych-stone or a wooden central coffin-rest has been removed in later times to allow a wheeled bier to pass through.

Lych-gates were in some districts built wholly of wood; in others, of wood on a stone base; but elsewhere entirely of stone. A few here and there are combined with a clerk's or sexton's cottage to form a gate house.

Ancient lych-gates were not very high, nor had they the ambitious scale or detail often seen in nineteenth-century and more recent versions. They were directly functional, and depended for their beauty on simplicity, proportion and good craftsmanship, never seeming to be in architectural competition with the church itself. Good Victorian architects saw the lych-gate as an integral part of the wall surrounding the churchyard; and the inter-relationship between them (and also between lych-gate, wall and the church itself) is often of considerable aesthetic importance.

In designing a new gate, consideration should be given to its function. It should be made of sufficient depth – at least 7 feet (2.134 m) – and of sufficient width to accommodate the coffin-bearers. The height is also of importance if vehicles are to pass through. In materials it should follow local traditions, being made of stone in a stone district and wood or brick where these prevail, with a roof-covering to harmonise with the church. In design it is reasonable to look for ancient precedents, but this need not entail a recreation of the past. What is important is a respect for local traditions and for context. In any event a faculty will be needed and the Diocesan Advisory Committee should be consulted at an early stage. In many country parishes, a well-placed tree near the church gate may afford shelter as effectively as a lych-gate.

In providing access for invalids, it is not desirable to place concrete ramps over the steps into the churchyard; an alternative entrance is the best solution.

In repairing ancient lych-gates care should be taken to preserve all original material and to follow the techniques of the original builders. This is specialist work, which needs to be supervised by a sensitive architect. Many lych-gates are spoiled by straightfor-ward neglect. Lamps need replacing or repairing from time to time. Advice on preservative treatment for old wood, and on the pointing of brick and stone should be obtained from the parish architect, the Diocesan Advisory Committee, the Council for the Care of Churches, or the Society for the Preservation of Ancient Buildings. Readers wishing to learn more about old lych-gates in their various forms are referred to the standard work on the subject, now more than half a century old, Aymer Vallance's *Old Crosses and Lychgates* (Batsford, 1920).

Part II
Legal Considerations

5

The General Legal Framework for the Care of Churchyards

INTRODUCTION

It is impossible in a short space to give an exhaustive account of the whole of the law affecting churchyards and what follows can do no more than indicate the main features. It is important to remember that the law is quite frequently changed by Acts of Parliament, by Orders made by government departments or by the decisions of the courts. Law relating to the Church of England may be changed by Measures passed by the General Synod and approved by Parliament. In any case of doubt, legal advice should be sought either privately from a solicitor or from the Diocesan Registrar who will have the necessary specialised knowledge. Practical advice may also be obtained from the Diocesan Secretary.

The legal ownership of a churchyard is usually vested in the incumbent, but both his own rights and his own obligations in respect of it are very limited. On the other hand, churchyards are the subject of rights and obligations affecting numerous persons. Some of the law applies in a similar manner to other pieces of land, but some relates specifically to church property or uniquely to churchyards. This chapter will consider briefly the major considerations of the general law relating to the care and maintenance of churchyards and also the legal considerations which arise when it is proposed to extend an existing churchyard or to open a new one. The following four chapters deal with the legal regulation of burials, including provision for new tombstones, the special aspects of secular law relating to the amenity of churchyards, the legal role of local authorities with regard to them, and the legal position of churchyards which are closed or which are attached to redundant churches. The English churchyard is traditionally thought of as a feature of the country village or small town. However, churchyards, or open spaces around churches in the inner city, can be of great value to the community. At the end of chapter 9 there is a brief summary of the legal aspects of the inner-city churchyard.

A NOTE ON CHURCHYARDS IN WALES

This handbook is about churchyards of the Church of England. The Church in Wales was disestablished by the Welsh Church Act 1914, and therefore Measures of the Church of England do not apply to it. However, the general legal principles outlined here will apply to Welsh churchyards just as they do to those in England. Similarly, the secular planning law described in chapter 7 applies in Wales, including the special exemption from listed building control for ecclesiastical buildings in use. Under the Welsh Church (Burial Grounds) Act 1945, Welsh churchyards are mainly the responsibility of the centralized Representative Body of the Church in Wales, although some churchyards have been transferred to local authorities. The Welsh system of local government differs somewhat from that in England, in particular having community councils instead of secular parish councils, and being under the general supervision of the Secretary of State for Wales, rather than of the Secretary of State for the Environment. The Church in Wales has its private courts which exercise a faculty jurisdiction similar to that of the English consistory courts. The Faculty Regulations and the special Churchyard Regulations of the Church in Wales, together with any further help needed with regard to Welsh churchyards, may be obtained from the Secretary General of the Church in Wales in Cardiff.

JURISDICTION OVER CHURCHYARDS

In the case of the ordinary parish church, the churchyard, like the church, is subject to the jurisdiction of the Bishop, exercised by the Chancellor in the Consistory Court. By an express provision of the Faculty Jurisdiction Measure 1964 this applies equally to the unconsecrated curtilage of a consecrated church, such as the grassed or paved area around many city or town churches built in the nineteenth or twentieth centuries, which have never had a burial ground.[1] Some modern places of worship may have been dedicated rather than consecrated. These and the land attached to them will only be subject to the faculty jurisdiction if the Bishop has expressly ordered.[2]

Where the faculty jurisdiction applies, no alterations, whether by way of addition, subtraction or otherwise, may be effected without a faculty from the court, save in the case of very minor works which can properly be regarded as *de minimis*. Certain uncontroversial matters, such as repairs and redecoration of a church, may be dealt with by an Archdeacon's Certificate.[3] However, this simplified procedure is not intended for alterations to the appearance of a church and will not be appropriate for changes in the churchyard. Thus, no electric cables or wires for lighting or heating may be laid in the ground or carried overhead without a faculty; nor, without a faculty, may pipes or storage-tanks for oil or water be installed; nor may any building be erected or removed. A faculty is also required for any substantial alteration in the layout of the churchyard, including the large-scale levelling of grave-mounds (though not individual cases), the removal or re-siting of grave-stones, the making of new paths or the removal of old ones, and the demolition or construction of walls or the substitution of one type of wall or fence for another. In certain circumstances, a faculty may be granted for the use of a churchyard for some secular purpose, such as the grant of a right of way to enable a neighbouring land-owner to obtain access to his property.

There are also statutory provisions under which monuments in a churchyard, indeed a whole churchyard, may be given special protection under secular law, notably by 'listing' under the Town and Country Planning Act 1971, or 'scheduling' under the

Ancient Monuments and Archaeological Areas Act 1979. The extent of secular control over churchyards and monuments and its relationship with the faculty jurisdiction are dealt with in greater detail in chapter 7.

CARE AND MAINTENANCE

The responsibility for maintaining the churchyard in good condition rests on the PCC, save in the case of a burial ground which has been closed by Order in Council and where the obligation has been passed to the local authority.[4] (The role of local authorities and the legal position of closed churchyards generally are dealt with further in chapters 8 and 9). It is important to note that local authorities and other public bodies may be able to help financially with churchyards which remain the responsibility of the PCC.

Canon F13 requires the churchyard to be fenced and kept 'in such an orderly and decent manner as becomes consecrated land'. The PCC's obligation is limited by the funds at its disposal. However, if a dangerous situation develops, there may be liability towards any visitor to the churchyard who is injured, even though remedying the danger would have been expensive.

It should be noted that the PCC's responsibility for the upkeep of the burial ground refers to the churchyard as a whole and the PCC may be liable for injury caused by an unsafe tombstone. The incumbent and PCC must also bear in mind the protection which these may be afforded under the secular law discussed in chapter 7. Individual tombstones remain primarily the responsibility of those who erected them, and after their death (according to the view most commonly accepted) of the heirs-at-law of those commemorated. As explained below, account must be taken of those with possible legal interests when it is proposed to remove an old tombstone. Often, however, such persons are not interested or cannot be traced; nor is there any enforceable legal obligation on them to maintain a memorial, save perhaps in the event of its becoming so dangerously ruinous as to constitute a danger to the public. Hence there is justice in requiring a donation towards the upkeep of the churchyard as a condition of the grant by faculty of any special privilege, such as the reservation of a grave space. Conversely, where a local authority has assumed responsibility for maintenance of a churchyard, the PCC sometimes pays a voluntary contribution.

It is open to anyone to give money on trust for the upkeep of the churchyard as a whole, though not on trust for the upkeep of a particular grave. A gift of money on trust for the upkeep of the churchyard as a whole, so long as a particular grave is maintained, is a valid charitable gift (however, specimen forms will be found in Appendix III). In such a case, the donor should give or bequeath a capital sum sufficient to provide an adequate annual income for the purpose; but the actual cost of maintaining the particular grave must be met from other sources, as if it is met from the income of the trust fund itself income tax exemption will be lost.

LITTER IN CHURCHYARDS

Litter, small and large, tends to get thrown into churchyards because of proximity to the highways. The law, as contained in the Litter Act 1983, makes it a punishable offence for anyone to deposit litter without proper authority 'into or from any place in the open air to which the public are entitled to have access without payment'. A churchyard is such a place, even if the gates are temporarily locked.

Further protection is given by the Refuse Disposal (Amenity) Act 1978, which forbids the deposit of larger objects such as cars, refrigerators, cookers, and washing machines which regrettably may be found in churchyards, particularly in some industrial areas. Under Section 3, a local authority is required to remove and dispose of cars abandoned in such circumstances and is empowered to help by removing other abandoned items. The local authority for these purposes is the District Council or, in London, the London Borough Council or the Common Council of the City. It should be noted that both the Litter Act and the Refuse Disposal (Amenity) Act require any prosecution to be begun by laying an information within six months of the alleged offence.[5]

Confetti is a problem in many churchyards, particularly where there are gravel paths and the paper is trodden in. The 'proper authority' in charge of a churchyard is the incumbent and churchwardens, who may permit or forbid it as they please. Outside the churchyard gates the responsibility and choice is that of the local highway authority. Where the practice has been traditional for years, and is not specifically forbidden, there is not likely to be a restriction.

HERBAGE AND TREES

The incumbent has the right of herbage in the churchyard. Thus, the grass which is cut therein belongs to him. Advantage is taken of this right all too seldom, for it may lawfully be exercised by turning sheep into the churchyard, and this, when done with discretion, is an admirable way of keeping down grass. Provided damage is not done to the monuments or flowers on new graves, and the rights of access to the church are not prejudiced, there would seem no reason why other animals, such as tethered goats, should not be used for this purpose.

Trees, however, unless dangerous, may not be felled without permission except to avoid some imminent risk. In this instance the permission is to be sought, not from the Consistory Court, but from the Parsonages Board of the diocese (or where there is no Parsonages Board, from the Diocesan Board of Finance) under Section 20 of the Repair of Benefice Buildings Measure 1972. The Faculty Jurisdiction Commission has recommended that it would be better if in future approval for felling should be granted under an Archdeacon's Certificate. At present the Diocesan Board may require the incumbent to fell timber as a matter of good management and should have a policy on this so as to ensure that the amenity of the churchyard is preserved. Since the character of many churchyards is greatly influenced by trees this method of control is an important safeguard. Where trees are felled, the Diocesan Board should require replanting as a matter of good management. Care should be taken, in particular, to avoid damaging ancient yew trees, which are irreplaceable and provide outstanding features, often with interesting historical associations.

Trees in a churchyard may be subject to Tree Preservation

Orders imposed by the local authority, and in a Conservation Area the consent of the local authority to lop or fell is also required. These restrictions are discussed further in chapter 7. Local authorities are often willing to give useful advice about maintenance and choice of species and siting for the planting of replacement trees. Particular care must be taken if new trees are planted, or grow after self-seeding, to ensure that they do not damage buildings or drains or cause other harm which could result in legal proceedings being brought against the church authorities. Such liability is possible if a tree's branches or roots extend beyond the boundary of the churchyard. It should also be remembered that removing trees on certain soil may cause the ground to heave or expand and cause damage.

OCCUPIERS' LIABILITY

Occupiers of land, and others with obligations in respect of land, always run the risk of incurring liability for damages towards persons who are injured by reason of hazards on the land, for example, a trench or open grave which has been inadequately fenced, a path or gravestone in dangerous condition, loose masonry on the church building, or a churchyard wall which has been faultily constructed or inadequately maintained. The responsibility of occupiers is provided for in the Occupiers' Liability Acts 1957 and 1984.

The occupier of land is the person who exercises control over it. In the case of a churchyard, this will certainly include the incumbent. However, responsibility for any negligent injury to visitors in the churchyard may also be shared by the PCC, whether they are technically occupiers as well or not.[6] The PCC is responsible for generally keeping the churchyard in decent order and specifically for maintaining fences and walls.[7] For example, if the PCC were informed that a wall was leaning dangerously over a footpath and failed to authorise approval to be sought of warning notices, it could be liable to compensate anyone injured by the later fall of the wall.

Individual members of the PCC will not normally be personally liable in such circumstances. However, it is possible that a member may become aware of a defect which has not been noticed by anyone else. If that person unreasonably fails to notify the incumbent or the churchwardens and an accident occurs which would probably have been prevented if the matter had been raised, that individual might be personally liable. An individual member of the PCC will be responsible for his own negligent acts, for example, if he or she runs into someone whilst mowing the grass.

During a vacancy in a parish, or where there is a priest-in-charge, the Bishop might be held responsible as occupier, since at such a time he is technically the owner of the freehold. Where a closed churchyard has been transferred to the local authority, this will acquire the responsibilities of the occupier, but the incumbent and PCC may still bear a duty to take care against hazards where they maintain control, for example in respect of drains from the church building running into the churchyard.

The duty to keep a churchyard safe is owed by the occupier to visitors.[8] These include anyone who is properly there, for such purposes as attending a service, visiting a grave or looking at the church. The duty consists in taking 'such care as is reasonable to see that the visitor will be reasonably safe in using the premises' for the purposes for which he or she is there.[9] Special attention must be paid to the vulnerability of children to danger.[10]

A duty is also owed, although a rather less onerous one, to persons using a private or a public right to pass through the churchyard, for example under the National Parks and Access to the Countryside Act 1949.[11] This lesser duty also extends to those who may not be entitled to be in the churchyard at all, for example revellers using it as a short cut after the gates have been locked for the night. Here the duty is only owed to those whose presence in the vicinity ought reasonably to have been anticipated and does not extend to their property. It applies in respect of danger of which the occupier is aware or has reasonable grounds to be aware.[12] The duty may be discharged 'by taking such steps as are reasonable in all the circumstances of the case to give warning of the danger concerned or to discourage persons from incurring the risk'.[13]

Practical examples where steps should be taken to avoid danger in a churchyard include maintenance of all stonework. If a piece of stone from the church or a boundary wall or a tombstone falls on someone, a court will normally assume that the structure had not been properly maintained, unless the contrary is proved. By contrast, if a branch falls from a tree, a court will not normally assume that this should have been prevented unless it appears that the occupier knew that the tree was unsafe or if this would have been apparent to any casual observer.

Particular care should be taken to keep paths safe. Thus paved paths should be regularly inspected and projections or holes dealt with. Gravel paths should be kept level. Special care should be taken to avoid danger in exceptional weather conditions. Thus it is prudent to sand paths if they become treacherous in heavy frost, to guard against large falls onto paths of melting snow from roofs or branches, and to check roofs and trees after heavy gales. Special care must be taken to prevent harm from everyday but potentially lethal activities such as mowing grass or burning rubbish. Occupiers of a churchyard may also be responsible for any nuisance affecting neighbouring land, for example if a wall collapses outwards onto it or onto the highway, or if harmful seeds spread onto an adjacent garden or farmland.

Even where funds are not immediately available to deal with a dangerous situation, such as an unsafe monument, it is vital that steps are taken to fence off any area of risk and to provide adequate warnings. However it must be stressed that, except in the short term, warning notices are no substitute for thorough remedial action. In particular, special care is owed to young children, who may be unable to read or understand warnings. Notices are of limited value in excluding liability.[14] They are also likely to be unsightly and may even attract vandals. In an emergency, remedial action may need to be taken immediately and a confirmatory faculty sought afterwards. In some dioceses the Chancellor permits gravestones which are leaning dangerously to be laid flat without a faculty.

INSURANCE

In view of their extensive responsibilities in the event of any accident occurring in the churchyard, it is essential to see that the incumbent and the PCC are adequtely covered by insurance against the damages which might be awarded in the event of an accident. It is particularly important to ensure that appropriate insurance has been taken out to cover any accidents in the church or churchyard which may result from work by church staff or members, or which may be caused by contractors. The typical church insurance policy provides indemnity for negligence, or under the Occupiers' Liability Acts where liability is proved. However, the insured will be required to take all reasonable precautions to avoid danger, must take immediate steps to remedy any defect which is discovered, and must cause such temporary precautions to be taken as the circumstances may require. If there is no incumbent it should be checked that the policy will cover any liability of the Bishop. An indemnity of not less than £1 million for any one occurrence should be effected.

Although a builder, for example, may be directly liable to anyone whom he injures, the occupier of the land on which he was working may also be liable, and may end up having to pay the compensation unless able to rely directly on an insurance policy. A form is given in Appendix III(i) which may be used to try and ensure that there is adequate insurance cover in the case of work carried out by a monumental mason in the churchyard. If such a form is to be used, it may be wise to provide a copy for those applying for permission to erect a monument at the same time as the form which is required for permission to erect the monument. For a model for this form see Appendix III(b).

USE FOR SECULAR PURPOSES

A faculty cannot authorise the complete alienation of a consecrat-ed churchyard. It is not permissible to sell or lease consecrated land. The only way in which alienation can be achieved is by statutory authority, e.g. by a scheme made under the Pastoral Measure 1983, as discussed in chapter 9, or a compulsory purchase order made under the Town and Country Planning Act 1971, Part VI.[15] However, so long as the land is not put to a use which is inconsistent with the act of consecration, a faculty may authorise parts of churchyards to be put to some appropriate and desirable secular use. For example, local authorities and others have been allowed to put lamps in the churchyard, to construct paths across it and lay drains and pipes for water, gas or electric cables under it, and to provide overhead wires for telephone or electricity, in some cases where the church or neighbouring land-owners will benefit. In certain cases, faculties have been granted to authorise the incumbent to license a neighbour with a right of access to his property or emergency egress from it, e.g. in the case of fire. Such licences are granted for specific periods or until further order. Faculties are also granted permitting a strip of churchyard to be incorporated into the highway for road-widening purposes.

RIGHTS OF WAY AND WAYLEAVES

No right of way, public or private, can exist in law over consecrated ground unless the dedication or grant is authorised by a faculty, but in appropriate cases, when the way has been used for a long time, the grant may be presumed of a faculty which has been lost. Some footpaths through churchyards have been recorded by local authorities as rights of way on Definitive Maps, originally provided under the National Parks and Access to the Countryside Act 1949, and now under the Wildlife and Country-side Act 1981.[16] If they are notified of any proposal for a revision which could affect their churchyard, an incumbent and the PCC should take all possible steps to ensure that no footpaths are erroneously recorded over the churchyard or there may be much confusion in the future.

Where the public are permitted to use footpaths through a churchyard as a matter of grace, it is important to take adequate steps to prevent a presumption of dedication arising. This can be done by closing the footpath one day a year or by exhibiting a notice in the churchyard or by depositing a plan with the local authority under the Highways Act 1980, Section 31. If the method of depositing a plan is used, care must be taken to follow it up by a statutory declaration every six years.

Similarly if the Area Electricity Board or British Telecom

desire to erect poles in the churchyard, application should be made for a faculty to do so. The erection of poles can easily spoil the amenities of the churchyard and it may well be that if the matter is dealt with in this way, some alternative position for them will be found. The local authority may in any case require this if the churchyard forms part of a Conservation Area. The laying of cables or drains, of course, requires a faculty.

Apart from problems arising where rights are claimed over a churchyard, difficulties may occur over access to the churchyard itself through neighbouring property. Thus where dioceses follow a policy of selling off large rectories and vicarages next to churches, it is vital to ensure that adequate rights are retained for access to the church and churchyard.[17] (The importance of providing for access in the case of disused churches or churchyards is further discussed in chapter 9). If provision needs to be made for access to a church or if any question arises of a right being created over a churchyard, it is particularly important to seek legal advice.

EXTENSIONS TO CHURCHYARDS AND NEW CHURCHYARDS

If an existing churchyard becomes full or if a new church is being provided, the question may arise as to whether the parish has an obligation to provide an extension or a new churchyard. There are powers to provide new land for burials, but as the acquisition of land is likely to be costly such a step should only be taken after careful deliberation. In the case of a new church, there does not seem to be any necessity to provide a burial ground. As explained in the next chapter, parishioners have a right to burial in an existing churchyard. When it becomes full, rather than extending it, the normal course today is to rely upon the local authority to provide ground for burials, if possible next to the churchyard. An application may be made to the Privy Council for the churchyard itself to be formally closed under the procedures discussed in chapter 9. Where a burial ground has been formally closed by an order in Council, the rights of burial for deceased parishioners are extinguished.

In parts of London and other large conurbations, it has long been impracticable for the church authorities to acquire expensive land to provide new burial grounds and the responsibility for doing so has been left to the secular burial authorities. In less built-up areas, particularly ones where the population is increasing with new housing expansion, similar problems are frequently likely to occur. If it is decided to extend the churchyard or to open a new one, land may be acquired for this purpose by the Church Commissioners under the New Parishes Measure 1943.[18] The Measure does not only apply to new parishes. The land acquired vests in the incumbent.[19] Although the Church Commissioners will deal with the acquisition, the purchase price will normally have to be found by the parish.

One situation where land may be obtained is where a parishioner, perhaps a farmer with a field next to the churchyard, is prepared to donate it. If he does so, he may reserve burial rights in it for his own family. Alternatively, it may be possible for glebe to be made available by the Diocesan Board of Finance, subject to the approval of the Church Commissioners,[20] or it may be possible for other land, such as part of the parsonage garden, to be sold or exchanged for land needed for a churchyard, subject to approval which will normally be required of both the Church Commissioners and the Bishop.[21] Rather than extending the churchyard, it may be more appropriate for church land, such as glebe, to be sold to the local authority for the provision of a suitable cemetery.

Where a new churchyard is opened or land is added to an existing one, planning consent will be required under the Town and Country Planning Act 1971. This is further discussed in chapter 7. In such cases there are special requirements for publishing details of the proposals so that any person concerned about them may have an opportunity to object.[22]

It should be borne in mind that provision may be made for the consecration of parts of secular cemeteries and also that local authorities have some powers to provide extra land for church-yards. Local authorities may site their own burial grounds near to the local parish church or next to an existing churchyard. However, it is important to avoid the character of a traditional churchyard being damaged or indeed overwhelmed by the proximity of a secular cemetery where controls over the quality of monuments will be less strict, especially if the cemetery is large. The involvement of local authorities in the provision of burial grounds is further discussed in chapter 8.

REGISTERS AND RECORDS

There are legal requirements for a parish to maintain a number of documents relating to the churchyard, and others should be kept as a matter of good practice.

The Inspection of Churches Measure 1955 provides for five-yearly inspections of each church in every diocese to be carried out by an approved diocesan architect. Between such inspections, a *Log Book* should be kept of work done to the church.[23] This should include a record of any work done on notice-boards, gates, walls, fences, or paths in the churchyard, with brief details of the work carried out, including the name and address of any architect or contractor involved.

Under Canon F16 the incumbent and churchwardens are required to keep an updated *Terrier and Inventory* of the possessions of the church. The terrier, from the French *terre,* meaning, 'land', relates to the land belonging to the church, rights which others may have over it and rights against neighbouring land. It should specify, for example, any rights of way, and may include details of noteworthy gravestones. The inventory relates to the contents of the church. It should list other documents, plans or registers, relating to the churchyard, which are kept at the church. A standard format for a combined terrier and inventory may be obtained from Church House Publishing.

A register of stones and inscriptions in churchyards is not currently required by law. However, it has been recommended by the Faculty Jurisdiction Commission that each parish should be required by law to keep a plan of the graves in the churchyard. The Commission has stressed that it is desirable to maintain much fuller records.[24] Advice on compiling such records, and keeping them up to date, including the use of filing cards, is given in chapter 6, and in appendices IV and V.

There is a legal requirement for the minister conducting a

burial to enter it, as soon as possible after the burial, in a Burial Register.[25] There is no such strict legal requirement in respect of the burial of cremated remains, or of a funeral where the committal has taken place in a local authority cemetery, because the official registration of the disposal of the body will have taken place at the crematorium or cemetery.[26] However, it is proper that a parish should have some record of the parishioners whose cremated remains have been buried in the churchyard. Indeed it is also helpful if a register is kept at a church of funerals and memorial services which have been conducted there, where neither the body nor cremated remains have been buried in the churchyard, including details of the burial or other form of disposal. This may, in particular, assist relatives and others who are looking for a grave in the churchyard of someone who is not interred there.

The importance of preserving all registers, plans and other documents, cannot be too strongly emphasised. Whether or not there is a specific legal requirement to keep such records, the churchwardens have legal ownership of them as trustees and are legally responsible for their proper care.[27] Church registers and other records are recognised as public and national records of the highest value. Good ink should always be used and never a ball-point pen. If the safe containing records shows signs of dampness, a drying agent, such as silica gel, may be kept in it. It is also wise to open the safe frequently in dry weather and to swing the door a few times to circulate the air. The books should be taken out occasionally for dusting and airing.

The Parochial Registers and Records Measure 1977 introduced important new arrangements for church records. Unless the Bishop gives express permission for them to be retained at the church, those which have been completed for 100 years must be deposited in the Diocesan Record Office for safe keeping and public access.[28] This office will have been nominated by the Bishop and will usually be a local authority record office. With the consent of the PCC, the churchwardens may deposit other records in the Diocesan Record Office, provided they are not in current use.[29] It may be useful to remember that the Diocesan Record Office may hold documents of relevance to the churchyard which do not come from the parish. For example, there may be papers relating to faculty applications originally compiled by the Diocesan Registrar, or plans of the churchyard made by local historians.

To summarise, old records relating to the churchyards should normally be deposited in the Diocesan Record Office. The following documents should be kept up to date at the church and should be carefully looked after:

1. The Church Log Book for repairs and alterations.
2. The Terrier and Inventory.
3. The register of stones and inscriptions.
4. The Burial Register.

NOTES

[1] Faculty Jurisdiction Measure 1964, Section 7(1).

[2] *Ibid,* Section 6(1).

[3] *Ibid,* Section 12.

[4] Local Government Act 1972, Section 214(1) and (8) and Schedule 26, and Local Authorities etc. (Miscellaneous Provisions) Order 1974, SI 1974, No. 482, Articles 15 and 16.

[5] Magistrates' Courts Act 1980, Section 127.

[6] The PCC succeeded to the responsibilities of the Churchwardens under the Parochial Church Councils (Powers) Measure 1956, Section 4(1)(ii)(c).

[7] Canon F13 and Parochial Church Councils (Powers) Measure 1956, Section 4(1)(ii)(c).

[8] Occupiers' Liability Act 1957, Sections 1 and 2.

[9] *Ibid,* Section 2(2).

[10] *Ibid,* Section 2(3)(a).

[11] National Parks and Access to the Countryside Act 1949, Section 60(1).

[12] Occupiers' Liability Act 1984, Section 1(3).

[13] *Ibid,* Section 1(5).

[14] Unfair Contract Terms Act 1977, Section 2.

[15] See in particular Town and Country Planning Act 1971, Section 128.

[16] Wildlife and Countryside Act 1968, part III.

[17] See *St. Edmundsbury and Ipswich Diocesan Board of Finance* v. *Clark (No. 2)* [1975]1 W.L.R. 468.

[18] New Parishes Measure 1943, Section 13.

[19] *Ibid,* Section 16, as substituted by Church Property (Miscellaneous Provisions) Measure 1960, Section 6(2).

[20] Endowments and Glebe Measure 1976, Sections 15 and 23(1)(a) and (e). See also Burial Ground Act 1816.

[21] Consecration of Churchyards Act 1867, Section 4; Places of Worship Sites Act 1873; and New Parishes Measure 1943, Section 17, as substituted by Church Property (Miscellaneous Provisions) Measure 1960, Section 6(2).

[22] Town and Country Planning Act 1971, Section 26, and General Development Order 1977, Article 8(1).

[23] Inspection of Churches Measure 1955, Section 1.

[24] Faculty Jurisdiction Commission Report, paragraph 314, Church House Publishing 1984.

[25] Parochial Registers and Records Act 1978, Sections 1 and 3.

[26] Local Authorities' Cemeteries Order 1977, SI 1977 No. 204, Art 11, as substituted by Local authorities' Cemeteries (Amendment) Order 1986, SS 1986 No. 1782.

[27] Revised Canons Ecclesiastical, Canon E1, paragraph 4.

[28] Parochial Registers and Records Measure 1977, sections 7 and 10(3).

[29] *Ibid,* sections 10(1)(32) and 11.

6

Legal Regulation of Burials and Monuments

By the Common Law, parishioners and persons dying in the parish have the right (through their personal representatives) to burial in the churchyard, if consecrated, if there is room, and if it has not been wholly closed for burials by Order in Council. By Section 6(1) of the Church of England (Miscellaneous Provisions) Measure 1976, the same right is given to persons whose names were at the date of their deaths on the church electoral roll of their parishes. There is, however, no right to burial in any particular part of the churchyard unless a space has been reserved by faculty or where the land has been gifted to the churchyard on the terms that part will be reserved.[1] A faculty reserving a particular space may be granted conditional on an agreement being entered into to make suitable payment into general funds for the maintenance of the churchyard. Normally it is within the incumbent's discretion to choose the spot for each burial.

The right to burial is not confined to members of the Church of England. Subject to certain limitations as to the use of the Church of England burial service, it is the duty of the incumbent, after due notice, to conduct the burial of any parishioner or person dying within the parish. However, where there is a right to burial, any relative, friend or legal representative has the further right to require, on giving proper written notice in accordance with the Burial Laws Amendment Act 1880, that the burial shall take place in the churchyard either without any service at all or with a Christian (though non-Anglican) service conducted by someone of their choosing, for example, a minister of another denomination.[2]

CREMATED REMAINS

The legal right to burial strictly relates to burial of a body and not of cremated remains, but Canon B38 provides that, 'save for a good and sufficient reason the ashes of a cremated body should be interred or deposited, by a minister, in consecrated ground'.[3] Therefore when the body of a person with a right of burial has been cremated, the subsequent burial of the cremated remains in the churchyard, if desired, would normally follow as a matter of course. Although burials may be prohibited or restricted by Order in Council, it would seem that the interment of cremated remains may still take place, as this would not constitute a burial within the meaning of the Burial Act 1853 under which closing orders are made.[4] However, as such interment might cause concern, or indeed be undesirable, in a churchyard which has had to be closed, not only should a faculty be obtained before such an interment takes place, but if the local authority is responsible for the upkeep of the churchyard, it should as a matter of courtesy, be consulted. This is particularly desirable if it is intended to set aside a portion of the churchyard for the interment of cremated remains. If the local authority become liable to additional expense as a result of a scheme for disposing of cremated remains, it should be specially cited on the presentation of the petition for the faculty. The burial of cremated remains is dealt with in detail in chapter 13.

BURIAL OF NON-PARISHIONERS

Although in the case of persons who are not parishioners, nor on the electoral roll, nor die within the parish, there is no right to burial in the churchyard, permission (which may be given generally to cover a limited class, or particularly in individual cases) may be given by the incumbent for such burial. Such permission should be granted sparingly, for it infringes the rights of the parishioners for whose interment the churchyard is primarily intended. It is particularly important, therefore, to avoid giving any impression that this permission will automatically be given in return for a substantial payment. Provided, however, that ample grave space is available, there is no reason why such burials should not be allowed on payment of a suitable charge, bearing in mind that this payment will normally be applied towards the maintenance of the churchyard.

There has in the past been some doubt as to the person whose consent is required for the burial of non-parishioners, but this has now been resolved by Section 6(2) of the Church of England (Miscellaneous Provisions) Measure 1976, which provides that:

> No person, other than a person having a right of burial in the churchyard or other burial ground of a parish, shall be buried therein without the consent of the minister of the parish, but in deciding whether to give such consent the minister shall have regard to any general guidance given by the parochial church council of the parish with respect to the matter.

In this connection, it should be remembered that there are certain categories of persons, such as ex-parishioners, and non-parishioners with family graves or vaults in the churchyard, or who have close relatives buried there, who may be regarded as almost having a customary right of burial and who deserve special concern and consideration.

DEPTH OF GRAVES

There is no uniform provision throughout the country about the depth of graves and there will be many churchyards where there is no restriction on this. Since about 1908 the normal practice has been three feet (900 mm). However, where there is any possibility of any restrictions being in force, they should be ascertained and observed. The most common provision is that contained in Section 103 of the Towns Improvement Clauses Act 1847 which, where it is in force by incorporation in a local Act, means that no coffin may be buried without at least thirty inches (750 mm) of soil between the lid and the surface of the ground.

The approval of the Secretary of State for the Environment or his predecessors for the opening of a churchyard or an extension has in certain cases been granted subject to compliance with regulations which provide that no coffin should be buried in an unwalled grave within four feet (1200 mm) of the level of the ground. When a churchyard has been closed by an Order in Council which contains exceptions, the Order usually stipulates a depth of not less than four feet (1200 mm), but sometimes five feet (1500 mm), and the Order should be referred to. Finally, in some areas there is special provision in a local Act fixing a minimum depth applicable to all burial places in the area, though this is only likely to be found in urban areas.

DISINTERMENT OF BODIES

Once a body has been buried, it may not be disinterred without lawful authority. In cases where crime is suspected this may be given by the coroner.[5] Both the Pastoral Measure 1983 and secular planning legislation make provision for the disinterment of bodies in burial grounds affected by redundancy or planning schemes and for their reinterment elsewhere.[6] In all other cases a faculty is required as, for example, where it is desired to remove a body from one part of the churchyard to another, perhaps because it was buried by mistake in the wrong grave space; and, in addition to a faculty, a licence is required from the Home Secretary under Section 25 of the Burial Act 1857, unless the re-burial is in consecrated ground. The disinterment of cremated remains and their re-interment elsewhere, which is to be discouraged, even if practicable, is dealt with in Chapter 13.

RE-USE OF OLD GRAVES FOR FRESH BURIALS

As there is no right to burial in any particular part of the churchyard unless a space has been reserved by faculty or under the Consecration of Churchyards Acts 1867 and 1868, it follows that (subject to compliance with any requirements about the depth of graves, or of any Order in Council restricting burials to relatives of those already buried in a particular grave, which may apply to that particular churchyard), there is no legal objection to burial in a grave which has already been used, even though the person to be buried is not related to any of those already buried in that grave. But clearly this could cause distress if done indiscriminately, and in practice, especially if a tombstone has been erected, further burials in a grave will usually be confined to members of the same family. There may, however, be some grave spaces where it is many years since any burial took place, or where it is known that the person buried has no surviving relatives, and where therefore it might not be inappropriate to use the grave for the burial of someone unconnected with the person or persons already buried there. This will be easier if no tombstone has been erected.

There might be a portion of a churchyard which has not been used for burials for many years (and which has not been closed for burial by Order in Council) where it would be appropriate to seek a faculty to remove (and possibly re-site) all the gravestones and make the ground available for re-use for burials.

It is usual for a gap of at least 50 years to elapse between burial and re-burial. It would be wise before re-using such ground to consult the Commonwealth War Graves Commission, lest there should be any of their graves in the area.

Even where rights to grave spaces have been granted by faculty or reserved under the Consecration of Churchyards Acts 1867 and 1868, the effect of Section 8 of the Faculty Jurisdiction Measure 1964 is that unless they are renewed by faculty, all such rights cease one hundred years after the passing of the measure or, in the case of extensions or new grants by faculty, after the date of the faculty.

MONUMENTS

Burial does not confer a right to erect a tombstone or other monument and, strictly speaking, the erection of one without a faculty is unlawful. Though the practice varies according to local conditions from diocese to diocese, it is usual today for the Chancellor to delegate to the incumbent authority to permit erection of memorials which fall within the conditions as to size, shape and materials set out in his delegation. Written application for permission to erect a memorial should be made in the first instance to the incumbent. Many dioceses have their own standard application forms which should be used.

It is important that no order for a tombstone should be placed until it has been ascertained that permission for its erection will be granted and the inscription approved. Distress may occur to relatives who accept a standard agreement such as may be offered by some undertakers to cover the funeral and the erection of a memorial, when the form of the standard memorial proves unsuitable. On the other hand, if the incumbent's permission is not forthcoming for a particular monument, it is still open to the applicant to apply for a faculty, provided he is a person with sufficient legal interest to be a petitioner. This may be the case where relatives wish to erect a memorial which differs from the normal diocesan conditions. The incumbent may not be in a position to approve an unusual memorial, but if proper advice is obtained for the design, a faculty may well be granted. The standards laid down for a diocese by its Chancellor are intended to simplify the approval of normal memorials, not to deter good original designs. Chapters 10, 11 and 12 give practical advice on the form of new memorials.

The suggested Rules set out in Appendix I illustrate the scope of the authority to approve monuments which Chancellors may choose to delegate to incumbents. Appendix II offers guidelines to assist PCCs to formulate their own rules for governing the erection of memorials. It is essential to ensure that the rules so adopted are consistent with the terms of the authority delegated by the Chancellor to the incumbent. Appendix III includes model forms which may be provided for applicants who wish to obtain approval for the erection of a memorial in a churchyard, together with forms to deal with future upkeep of graves. As was seen in the preceding chapter, provision for the maintenance of a particular grave should be made through a trust in favour of the upkeep of the churchyard as a whole.

REMOVAL OR RE-SITING OF MONUMENTS

Where a memorial becomes dangerous or derelict, or where the space is required for a new grave, a faculty may be sought for its removal or re-siting. The appropriate method of disposal will vary depending on the form of the monument, the character of the churchyard and the nature of the soil. For example, in some circumstances it may be appropriate to bury old gravestones below the frost level, as in the right conditions this may preserve inscriptions cut on them. Removal from the churchyard should normally be avoided unless a tombstone or monument is assured of safe keeping elsewhere. A record should always be kept, and sent to the local records office, of any gravestone which is moved, with details of its original site, any inscription, and the method of disposal. Except in cases of necessity, gravestones should not normally be removed individually but should be dealt with as part of a general re-ordering scheme, when maintenance and aesthetic, archaeological and historical considerations may be dealt with thoroughly in a single faculty petition.

Where it is proposed to move, demolish, alter or otherwise carry out work on an existing monument, if the owner can be identified he or she must be given the opportunity under the faculty to remove the monument.[7] Before a faculty can be granted, the Chancellor must be satisfied that reasonable efforts have been made to find the owner. In practice, notice of the proposal should be published on the church notice-board, in the parish magazine and in one or more local newspapers. Enquiry should be made of any parishioners who might recall relatives, and any known relatives should be approached. If a relative does come forward, this may relieve the parish of expense. Generous time should be allowed for the giving of notice, certainly at least three months before the presentation of the faculty petition. A suggested form of advertisement is given in Appendix III(a).

FEES

Tables of fees, made by the Church Commissioners with the approval of the General Synod under the Ecclesiastical Fees Measure 1986, govern the amounts payable in respect of burials and the erection of monuments.[8] In addition to these, in those cases where a faculty is sought, for example, for the erection of a monument of a kind which might make it more difficult to keep the churchyard tidy, or for the reservation of a grave space, it has become customary in many dioceses for the court to grant such a faculty only on condition that an additional sum is paid to the parochial church council to help towards the upkeep of the churchyard. At present there is considerable variation in such sums, owing to different conditions in different parts of the country. Because of inflation, the sum agreed should be reviewed from time to time and indeed suggestions have been made for an annual rental. Parochial church councils should be encouraged to establish a Churchyard Maintenance Fund for the upkeep of the churchyard, into which these sums should be paid.

RECORDS AND BOOKS OF REMEMBRANCE

As explained at the end of chapter 5, there is a legal requirement for a parish to maintain records of burials which have taken place in the churchyard.[9] There is no strict requirement for a register of the burial of cremated remains, but it is proper that such a register should be maintained of the parishioners whose cremated remains have been buried in the churchyard. The record should contain (a) the full name of the deceased; (b) the former home address; (c) the date of burial; (d) the reference for the grave or other place of disposal in the churchyard; (e) the name of the officiating minister.

Books of Remembrance provide a very useful alternative to outdoor memorials on stone. The book should be handsome and strongly bound and housed in the church on a well-designed lectern or in a ventilated glass case. A faculty is required for the book itself and for the lectern or glass case. The Diocesan Advisory Committee should be consulted on design and position.

One advantage of such a book is that, whereas carved inscriptions must be short, it is possible to allow perhaps half a page for a full entry in the book, provided that appropriate payment is made for the calligraphy. Entries should be made by the same professional calligrapher so as to preserve uniformity of style. To the cost of writing should be added a small sum for the insurance and renewal of the book itself. Another advantage is that entries may be included of persons whose remains are not interred in the churchyard at all, for example where a parishioner has been lost at sea or has donated his body to medical research.

NOTES

[1] Consecration of Churchyards Act 1867, Section 9, as amended by Consecration of Churchyards Act 1868, Section 1.

[2] Burial Laws Amendment Act 1880, Sections 1 and 6.

[3] Canon B38, Paragraph 4 (b).

[4] Burial Act 1853, Section 1.

[5] Coroners' Act 1980, Sections 1 and 4.

[6] Pastoral Measure 1983, Section 65 and schedule 6; Town and Country Planning Act 1971, Section 128, and Town and Country Planning (Churches, Places of Religious Worship and Burial Grounds) Regulations 1950, SI 1950, No. 792.

[7] Faculty Jurisdiction Measure 1964, Section 3.

[8] See the Parochial Fees Order 1986, SI 1986, No. 1148.

[9] Parochial Registers and Records Measure 1978, Sections 1 and 3.

7

Secular Planning Control

GENERAL PLANNING CONTROL

It may be helpful to recapitulate the extent to which churches in use are affected by secular planning legislation. The legislation is mainly administered by local planning authorities, which are usually district councils, or London borough councils. There is provision for appeals on disputed decisions to the Department of the Environment, which also provides general supervision, notably by calling in controversial cases to be decided centrally. Contrary to what is sometimes supposed, churches are subject to ordinary planning control in 'the same way as most secular buildings. Planning permission is required for the carrying out of any development of land.[1]

Building works are treated as development unless they only affect the interior of an existing building or do not materially affect the exterior appearance of a building.[2] In other words, planning permission is required for material alterations to the exterior of a church. These may include any of the following:

(1) the substitution of a different form of roof-covering;

(2) the alteration of the external appearance of a window, e.g. by the provision of double glazing or grilles or by replacing a leaded window with a single sheet of glass;

(3) the addition of a porch or vestry;

(4) the installation of an outside oil storage tank;

(5) the addition or removal of a clock-dial, or of pinnacles or parapets on a tower or roof.

Planning permission will be required for any extension to a church building and also for permanent structures erected in the churchyard. These could include relatively modest additions such as a substantial notice-board. Substantial alterations to a churchyard in the form of levelling or recontouring could require planning permission as engineering operations. However, development does not include outright demolition of any building or smaller structure. Permission for demolition is normally only required from a local planning authority where a building is 'listed' or is in a Conservation Area. As is explained below, churches and churchyards are in a special position with regard to these forms of secular control.

A second major form of development consists of any material change in the use of any building or other land. This would include the incorporation of new land into a churchyard or the use of any separate land for burials or for the deposit of cremated remains.

THE 'LISTING' OF CHURCHES

Planning legislation has, since 1947, required the Secretary of State for the Environment or his equivalent to list buildings that are considered to be of special architectural or historic interest.[3] He employs a team of skilled investigators for that task. When a building is so listed it is normally necessary to obtain Listed Building Consent before the carrying out of any works for its demolition, or its alteration or extension in a way which materially affects its character as a building of special interest. Something like 12,000 churches belonging to the Church of England have been listed. These include virtually all medieval churches. The lists are being constantly revised so that, for example, an increasing number of nineteenth-century churches are now listed. However, ecclesiastical buildings for the time being used for ecclesiastical purposes are exempted from listed building control.[4]

A local planning authority may serve a Building Preservation Notice as a temporary means of conferring the protection obtainable from listing[5] and, under powers provided by the Town and Country Amenities Act 1974, local authorities may designate Conservation Areas which are of special architectural or historic interest. Buildings in such areas are protected from demolition unless consent is obtained.[6] However, the exemption is extended to cover these provisions as well, so that neither Building Preservation Notices nor the restrictions protecting buildings in Conservation Areas apply at present in respect of any ecclesiastical building for the time being used for ecclesiastical purposes.[7] In the event of outright demolition, a church will cease to be used for ecclesiastical purposes, so the exemption in its various forms does not apply.[8]

The reason for the exemption is the faculty jurisdiction, which is the Church of England's equivalent to secular listed building control. In some respects the faculty jurisdiction is more comprehensive and effective than listed building control. In particular it protects furnishings inside churches, whether moveable or otherwise. Also it protects churches and churchyards which have not been listed at all by the secular planning authorities. However, the exemption has recently been under attack by local planning authorities and by various conservation groups. These attacks seem partly to have resulted from a suspicion by some in local government of what they may see as a rival jurisdiction, and partly from confusion of the exemption with the quite separate provisions which govern the demolition of redundant Anglican churches. Listed building consent is not required for the demolition of the whole or part of a redundant church building in pursuance of a pastoral or redundancy scheme under the Pastoral Measure 1983.[9] A further reason for concern has been the fact that the exemption applies to non-Anglican churches, which lack the advantages of the faculty jurisdiction.

Now, under the Housing and Planning Act 1986, the Secretary of State for the Environment has been given power to make orders removing the exemption generally or in specific cases.[10] The government has stated in the House of Lords, through Lord Skelmersdale, the then Parliamentary Under-Secretary of State for the Department of the Environment, that no such order is expected to be made in respect of churches belonging to the Church of England.[11] However, the fact remains that the government could now abolish the exemption without the need for approval by an Act of Parliament. This would undermine the position of the faculty jurisdiction. If the protection of churches and churchyards were simply superseded by listed building control, the Church would lose the flexibility of the present system for approving experiments and changes suitable for living places of worship, and those concerned with conservation would lose a thorough system suited to protect the parish church, with its contents and in its setting, as part of the national heritage.

The detailed provisions of the faculty jurisdiction are at present being revised in a way that should make the system simpler where possible and more effective in balancing the insights of all who care about the important issues raised by proposed changes.[12] It is clear that if the benefits of the exemption are to be preserved, it is vital that the provisions of the faculty jurisdiction should be scrupulously observed in respect of both churches and church-yards.

At present, listing of churches is of some guidance to local authorities who may contribute, under the Local Authorities (Historic Buildings) Act 1962, towards the expenses incurred in the repair or maintenance of buildings of architectural or historic interest, including churches.[13] Where such grants are made, they may be conditional upon the local authority approving later alterations quite independently of its powers under listed building control.

CHURCHYARDS

Structures in churchyards may, like the churches, be listed by the Secretary of State. However, listing may have no legal effect if the church associated with the churchyard is listed on its own account and is in use for ecclesiastical purposes. This is because any object or structure is treated as part of a listed building if it has been within the curtilage of that building since before July 1948, when modern planning law was introduced.[14] Some at least of the land surrounding a church will be included in its curtilage. It is possible that if the Secretary of State makes an order under the Housing and Planning Act 1986, the position could be affected.

In any event, if a church is unlisted but a structure in the churchyard is listed on its own account, Listed Building Consent will be required before work is done to that structure. Similarly where the church is unlisted, a structure in the churchyard may be protected by a Building Preservation Notice. These provisions could provide protection for ancient or interesting features in the churchyard of an undistinguished church, such as the base of an old preaching cross or a lych-gate. Where the church is unlisted but the churchyard is in a Conservation Area, there is protection from demolition for substantial walls, of two metres, or adjacent to a highway, of one metre. Separate structures will also be protected from demolition if they are more than 115 metres in cubic content, such as a free-standing tower or barn.[15]

There are other controls which may apply to churchyards even though they do not apply to churches. Under the Ancient Monuments and Archaeological Areas Act 1979, the Secretary of State is empowered to schedule ancient monuments. It is an offence to damage or demolish or alter such a monument without the consent of the Secretary of State.[16] For the purposes of this Act, 'the expression "monument" includes any building structure or work whether above or below the surface of the land or any cave or excavation'.[17] If a listed building or a building in a Conservation Area is also scheduled as an ancient monument, the restrictions for protecting listed buildings or buildings in Conservation Areas are replaced by those for ancient monuments.[18] An ecclesiastical building in use for ecclesiastical purposes cannot be designated as an ancient monument, but structures in churchyards are eligible for scheduling.[19] The Secretary of State may therefore schedule such features as the following:

(1) Memorials and mausolea.

(2) Gates and boundary walls, and lych-gates.

(3) Sundials.

(4) Architectural fragments.

It is even possible for a whole churchyard, excluding the church, to be scheduled as an ancient monument. Alternatively, under the same Act, a churchyard or part of a churchyard may be designated as an area of archaeological importance.[20] In such a case, six weeks notice must be given to the District Council of any operations which will disturb the ground.[21]

A churchyard or part of a churchyard could also be notified by the Nature Conservancy Council as a site of special scientific interest, commonly known as an S.S.S.I., 'by reason of any of its flora, fauna, or geological or physiographical features'.[22] The effect of such notification is that it is an offence to carry out any operation which the Council has warned is likely to cause damage, unless agreement has been obtained from the Council or unless the Council has been given four months notice.[23] This time may be extended in certain cases especially where the site is of national interest. A churchyard or part of a churchyard could be notified as an S.S.S.I. so as to prevent the clearing of vegetation containing rare plant species.

BOUNDARY WALLS, ETC.

With regard to planning permission, gates, fences and walls are in a special category. Under the General Development Order their construction does not require planning permission so long as they do not exceed 1 metre in height where abutting on a highway used by vehicular traffic, or 2 metres high elsewhere.[24] However, in Conservation Areas a direction may be made which removes the exemption of such minor operations from the normal require-ments of planning permission.[25] Where such a direction has been made the construction of gates, fences and walls *would* require planning permission. The restrictions on fences and walls do not apply to hedges, even where these grow to a considerable height, although if a hedge is on a road junction it may be important to keep it trimmed low to ensure safe visibility for drivers.

TREES

Trees are distinguished from buildings in planning legislation. Those in churchyards enjoy no special status. A local planning authority may make a Tree Preservation Order, and where a tree is subject to such an Order it may not, except with the consent of the authority or under certain listed circumstances, be cut down, topped, lopped, uprooted or wilfully damaged or destroyed.[26] Similar protection applies to trees in a Conservation Area which has been created since the passing of the Town and Country Amenities Act 1974.[27] Where consent is given to fell a protected tree, a condition requiring replanting may be imposed. Where a hedge is of interest and consists of trees, it can be protected by means of a Tree Preservation Order.

The faculty jurisdiction does not provide protection for trees in churchyards in the same way that it does for church buildings and other structures. As discussed in chapter 5, the permission of the Diocesan Parsonages Board or Board of Finance is required before felling and should be sought before any substantial lopping. However, the Board's consent is not strictly required for lopping or topping of trees in the churchyard as it is in the case of those on land attached to the parsonage.[28] Therefore secular Tree Preservation Orders can provide much more substantial protection and it may be desirable for the PCC to ask the local planning authority to place a Tree Preservation Order on significant trees or groups of trees in the churchyard for the benefit of posterity. The relationship which may be developed with the landscape section of the local planning office may produce helpful advice on maintenance.

Even when there is not a Tree Preservation Order on a tree, it may be in the interests of good management of the churchyard to seek consent to fell. Indeed, as we have seen in chapter 5, the relevant Diocesan Board can give directions for the felling of trees in the churchyard provided they are not subject to a Tree Preservation Order or in a Conservation Area. When it is proposed to cut down an attractive tree, opposition is often misplaced. It may be important that mature trees should be felled before they pass their prime and decay sets in. Consent to fell from the local planning authority will usually require planting of a replacement. However, where there is proper foresight this will have been done a number of years in advance. Such foresight is necessary to mitigate the disaster caused by gales such as those which devastated many churchyards in the south of England in 1987.

A traditional alternative to felling which could be practised more widely today is pollarding. If a tree is subject to a Tree Preservation Order the consent of the local planning authority will still be required.

It should be stressed that Tree Preservation Orders are particularly appropriate for yew trees which are significant features of many churchyards. Some of these are over 1,000 years old and predate the church. Yews take a long time to become established and pose little threat to buildings. Even when they appear dead they often revive. If a yew or other tree is subject to a Tree Preservation Order, this should help to protect it from ill-considered lopping and from other abuse which, sadly, is by no means unknown, such as burning rubbish against the trunk.

NOTICE-BOARDS

Apart from the requirements of a faculty and of planning permission, notice-boards in the churchyard, and possibly in the church porch, are regulated by the Town and Country Planning (Control of Advertisements) Regulations 1984. Generally these require Advertisement Consent from the local planning authority for any new board or other form of notice which might be placed in a churchyard, apart from official notices by local authorities and other public bodies, certain temporary notices, including 'Advertisements announcing any local event of a religious, educational, cultural, political, social or recreational character', and small notices up to 0.2 square metres, 'displayed for the purpose of identification, direction or warning', with respect to the church or churchyard.[29] One permanent notice-board is permitted of up to 1.2 square metres. If the churchyard has entrances onto more than one road, a second board is permitted provided it is on a different frontage.[30]

To sum up. The effect of secular legislation on churchyards is as follows:

(i) Even though the church is unlisted, a structure in a churchyard may be protected by being listed in its own right. It will also be protected if it is of substantial size and is in a Conservation Area.

(ii) A local authority Building Preservation Notice may not be served in respect of a memorial or wall or other structure in a churchyard if the church itself is listed. In such cases it is essential that the faculty jurisdiction should afford protection equal to that of secular legislation.

(iii) Whether or not the church is listed, the scheduling as an ancient monument of a structure in a churchyard such as a lych-gate has statutory effect.

(iv) A local authority may make a Tree Preservation Order in respect of a tree or a hedge composed of trees in a churchyard. The whole or part of a churchyard may be scheduled as an ancient monument or notified as an S.S.S.I. or designated as an archaeological area.

(v) Planning permission may be required for partial demolition of a church or altering its exterior appearance, even though planning permission is not required for outright demolition. Building or rebuilding on the churchyard, recontouring the ground or even the erection of new structures other than modest boundary walls will require planning consent.

(vi) New notice-boards may require Advertisement Consent.

NOTES

[1] Town and Country Planning Act 1971, Section 23(1).

[2] *Ibid*, Section 22(2)(a).

[3] *Ibid*, Section 54(1).

[4] *Ibid*, Section 56(1)(a).

[5] *Ibid*, Section 58(1).

[6] *Ibid*, Section 277A(2) as inserted by Town and Country Amenities Act 1974, Section 1, and as modified by Town and Country Planning (Listed Buildings and Conservation Areas) Regulations 1987, SI 1987 No. 349.

[7] *Ibid*, Sections 58(2) and 277A(1)(b), as inserted by Town and Country Amenities Act 1974, Section 1.

[8] Attorney General v. Trustees of the Howard United Reformed Church, Bedford [1975] A.C. 363.

[9] Redundant Churches and Other Religious Buildings Act 1969, Section 2.

[10] *Ibid*, Section 58AA as inserted by Housing and Planning Act 1986, Section 40 and Schedule 9, paragraph 5.

[11] Parliamentary Debates, House of Lords, 22 Oct. 1986, cols 387-389.

[12] Following the Report of the Faculty Jurisdiction Commission under the Chairmanship of the Bishop of Chichester, 1984, CIO.

[13] Local Authorities (Historic Buildings) Act 1962, Section 1.

[14] Town and Country Planning Act 1971, Section 54(9), as amended by Housing and Planning Act 1986, Section 40 and Schedule 9, paragraph 1(1).

[15] *Supra,* note 6, as qualified by Department of the Environment Circular No. 8/87, paragraph 97.

[16] Ancient Monuments and Archaeological Areas Act 1979, Section 2.

[17] *Ibid,* Section 61(7).

[18] Town and Country Planning Act 1971, Sections 56(1), 58(2) and 277A(1)(b).

[19] For example, in one county alone (Staffordshire) there are 14 scheduled monuments, all of them crosses. It seems that the Secretary of State will use his powers in this respect with increasing frequency, to protect individual monuments or whole churchyards.

[20] Ancient Monuments and Archaeological Areas Act 1979, Section 33.

[21] *Ibid,* Section 35(1).

[22] Wildlife and Countryside Act 1981, Section 28(1).

[23] *Ibid,* Section 28(5) and (6).

[24] General Development Order 1977, SI 1977 No. 289 Schedule I, Class II.

[25] *Ibid,* Article 4 and Department of the Environment Circular No. 23/77, paragraphs 38 and 41.

[26] Town and Country Planning Act 1971, Section 60(1)(a), as amended by Local Government, Planning and Land Act 1980, Schedule 15, paragraph 13.

[27] *Ibid,* Section 61A as inserted by Town and Country Amenities Act 1974, Section 8.

[28] Repair of Benefice Buildings Measure 1972, Section 20(1).

[29] Town and Country Planning Act 1971, Section 63, and Town and Country Planning (Control of Advertisements) Regulations 1984, SI 1984 No. 421. Regulations 6 and 14, Classes I, III, and IIa. See also Town and Country Planning (Control of Advertisements) (Amendment) Regulations 1987, SI 1987, No. 804.

[30] Town and Country Planning (Control of Advertisements), Class II.

8

The Role of Local Authorities

ASSISTANCE FROM LOCAL AUTHORITIES

The Local Government Act 1972 provides that:

> A burial authority may contribute towards any expenses incurred by any other person in providing or maintaining a cemetery in which the inhabitants of the authority may be buried.[1]

'Burial authorities' are defined to include district councils, the councils of London boroughs, the Common Council of the City of London, and also parish councils and parish meetings of parishes having no parish council. In Wales such authorities include community councils.[2] 'Cemetery' includes a burial ground or any place for the interment of the dead (including any part of any such place set aside for the interment of a dead person's ashes.[3] This is a wide power which allows for local authority assistance in the upkeep of churchyards which are still in use.

Local authorities have a number of more specific powers which may enable them to help towards the upkeep of certain features of churchyards, and there are some central government funds available to supplement these through the Historic Buildings and Monuments Commission for England, commonly known as English Heritage.

ANCIENT MONUMENTS

County and district councils, London borough councils and the Common Council of the City of London have powers to contribute towards preserving and maintaining and managing structures in churchyards which are recognised as ancient monuments, under the Ancient Monuments and Archaeological Areas Act 1979.[4] Help may thus be provided for features such as memorials, mausolea, sundials, stocks and lych-gates. English Heritage has further power to contribute towards the expense of moving a monument so as to preserve it.[5]

WAR MEMORIALS

Under the War Memorials (Local Authorities Powers) Act 1923,[6] county and district councils and also parish councils and parish meetings of parishes without a parish council and community councils have power to incur reasonable expenditure on the maintenance, repair and protection of war memorials, whether vested in them or not. This power extends to incurring expenditure in altering a war memorial so as to make it serve as a memorial in connection with any later war.[7] Thus provision could be made for adapting a memorial from the first and second world wars, so as to commemorate the dead of more recent conflicts such as that in the Falkland Islands.

PUBLIC FACILITIES

Local authorities have general powers, under the Local Government Act 1972, to 'incur expenditure, which in their opinion is in the interests of their area or any part of it or all or some of its inhabitants'.[8] However, this catch-all power does not apply where there is other specific statutory authority for a particular purpose. A number of facilities which are provided for under such specific powers could be sited in a churchyard if it were thought appropriate to grant a faculty for them.

There are specific powers under the Public Health Acts for payments in respect of public clocks[9] and seats and drinking fountains.[10] Parish councils and meetings and community councils have similar powers, under the Parish Councils Act 1957, in respect of seats and shelters abutting a road,[11] clocks,[12] and lighting.[13] These general and specific powers of local authorities may be useful if help is sought for the maintenance or improvement of the curtilage of a church which has not been used for burials, as may often be the case with modern places of worship.

CARE AND MANAGEMENT OF A BURIAL GROUND

Under the Open Spaces Act 1906,[14] local authorities have power to agree to undertake the entire or partial care, management and control of a burial ground as such, that is without laying it out as an open space and while permitting burials to continue there. This would probably not be an appropriate provision under which to seek help for a churchyard surrounding a church in use, but it could be useful in the interests of amenity, or to prevent a scandal, where burials still take place but no funds or only inadequate funds are available for maintenance. This could be the case with a detached churchyard or one of the church burial grounds which were established in the nineteenth century for burials which had to be according to the rites of the Church of England.[15] Such assets as are available for general maintenance in such a case could be transferred to the local authority.[16]

The Open Spaces Act 1906 provides more extensive powers under which disused burial grounds, whether formally closed or not, may be transferred to a local authority to be improved and laid out as an open space for public use.[17] As explained in the next chapter, a churchyard, with or without the church building, may in certain circumstances be disposed of under the Pastoral Measure 1983, so that it ceases to be subject to the control of the faculty jurisdiction. This may be appropriate in the case of redundant churches of no particular historical or aesthetic note, especially in derelict urban areas. It may be appropriate to dispose of some or the whole of a churchyard whilst retaining the church, particularly if the churchyard is large or in a very run-down area.

Normally where a local authority even takes over the full maintenance and control of a churchyard under the Open Spaces Act 1906, the churchyard will not be permanently transferred but will be maintained by the local authority for a set time under an agreement. The Diocesan Registrar should be asked for advice on the form that this should take. Where a local authority acquires control of a churchyard on any basis under the Open Spaces Act

1906, Section 10 of the Act requires it to administer it with a view to enjoyment by the public as an open space under proper control and regulation. It must maintain the churchyard in a good and decent state and it has powers to provide proper railings and gates, drainage, turf, planting, ornaments, lights and seats, apart from generally levelling and laying out the ground as appropriate. A faculty will be required for such improvements and should be sought by the local authority.

CLOSED CHURCHYARDS

In the case of churchyards closed for burials by Order in Council (whether with or without exceptions permitting certain burials to take place) the Local Government Act 1972 provides that the PCC shall maintain the churchyard by keeping it in decent order and its walls and fences in good repair.[18] However, here, the PCC may transfer the obligation to the appropriate local authority by serving a written request to that effect.[19] The request may be served upon the parish council or meeting or community council if there is one and otherwise on the district or London borough council in whose area the churchyard will be transferred three months after the serving of the request.[20] A parish council or meeting or community council served with such a request may, within the three months, transfer the responsibility to the district council.

Because of the need for local authorities to budget for future commitments, it is normal practice to give informal notice twelve months before serving a formal request on a local authority to maintain a churchyard. Where responsibility for the maintenance of a closed churchyard had been transferred to a local authority before April 1974 under the old law, the future responsibility for its maintenance now rests upon the local authority upon whom a request would have fallen to be served.[21]

It should be stressed that, unless it has been disposed of under the provisions of the Pastoral Measure 1983, which are discussed in the next chapter, a closed churchyard remains subject to the faculty jurisdiction, and even though responsibility for maintenance is transferred to the local authority, it may still be used for church purposes. The incumbent may still claim his right to herbage. Where the local authority proposes to carry out improvements, it should be responsible for the necessary faculty. If a faculty is sought by the incumbent and PCC for some purpose which may impose extra financial liability on the local authority, such as the allocation of a landscaped area for the disposal of cremated remains, the local authority should be specially cited, and thus formally notified in writing of the proposal, with the opportunity to object.

PROVISION OF NEW LAND FOR CHURCHES

Secular burial authorities, defined under the Local Government Act 1972, are district councils, London borough councils, and also parish, or, in Wales, community councils, or in a case where there is no parish council, the parish meeting.[22] Burial authorities have the power to provide their own burial grounds.[23] If they are district councils or London borough councils they may acquire land for burials, either by agreement[24] or under powers of compulsion, subject to the approval of the Secretary of State.[25] They may also appropriate for burial grounds land which they hold for other purposes for which it is no longer required.[26]

A burial authority may seek consecration of part of a secular cemetery, but it must ensure that a sufficient part of the cemetery remains available for general use and is not consecrated.[27] Thus a burial authority may in appropriate circumstances provide a secular cemetery adjacent to an old churchyard, or a newly created church, and confer supervision over part of it to the church authorities by seeking consecration of that part. Such a part could be physically separated from the remainder of the cemetery, for example by a hedge and trees or by more substantial landscape features.[28] With mutual co-operation, church land, such as glebe, may be sold to the local authority, and the local authority may bear the expense of landscaping, erecting fences, and maintenance.[29]

If a local authority, whether it is a burial authority or not, is prepared to assist a church by providing land for a new churchyard or a churchyard extension, under the Places of

Worship Acts 1873 and 1882, it may provide, with or without payment, any number of permanent sites of up to one acre each, subject to the approval of the Secretary of State.[30]

A secular burial ground or part of one, or other local authority land, could also be transferred to a church under general powers of disposal vested in local authorities. However, unless such land is transferred under a short tenancy of not more than seven years or the consent of the Secretary of State is obtained, the church would be required to pay the market value for the land.[31]

NOTES

[1] Local Government Act 1972, Section 214 (6).

[2] *Ibid*, Section 214 (1).

[3] *Ibid*, Section 214 (8).

[4] Ancient Monuments and Archaeological Areas Act 1979, Section 24 (4).

[5] *Ibid*, Section 24 (2), as amended by National Heritage Act 1983, Schedule 4, paragraph 48.

[6] War Memorials (Local Authorities Powers) Act 1923, Section 1, as amended by Local Government Act 1948, Section 133 (1).

[7] Local Government Act 1948, Section 133 (2).

[8] Local Government Act 1972, Section 137 (1).

[9] Public Health Act 1875, Section 165, as extended by Public Health Act Amendment Act 1890, Section 46.

[10] Public Health Act 1925, Section 14.

[11] Parish Councils Act 1957, Section 1.

[12] *Ibid*, Section 2.

[13] *Ibid*, Section 3.

[14] Open Spaces Act 1906, Section 9(b).

[15] See Halsbury's Laws of England, Fourth Edition, 1975, volume 10, title 'Cremation and Burial', paragraph 1073, note 1.

[16] Parish Councils and Burial Authorities (Miscellaneous Provisions) Act 1970, Section 1.

[17] Open Spaces Act 1906, Sections 6, 9(a), and 10.

[18] Local Government Act 1972, Section 215 (1).

[19] *Ibid*, Section 215 (2).

[20] *Ibid*, Section 215 (3).

[21] Local Government Act 1972, Section 214(1) and (8) and Schedule 26, and Local Authorities etc. (Miscellaneous Provisions) Order 1974, SI, 1974, No. 482, Articles 15 and 16.

[22] Local Government Act 1972, Section 214(1) and (5).

[23] *Ibid*, Section 214(2).

[24] *Ibid*, Section 120.

[25] *Ibid*, Section 121.

[26] *Ibid*, Section 122.

[27] Local Authorities Cemetery Order 1977, SI 1877, No. 204, Article 5.

[28] *Ibid*, Art. (5)4.

[29] Endowment and Glebe Measure 1976, Section 20, and New Parishes Measure 1943, Section 17, as substituted by Church Property (Miscellaneous Provisions) Measure 1960, Section 6(2).

[30] Places of Worship Sites Act 1882, Section 1, and Places of Worship, Sites, Amendment, Act 1882, Section 1. See too Transfer of Functions (Places of Worship, Sites) Order 1953, SI 1953, No. 734, and the Secretary for State for the Environment Order 1970, SI 1970, No. 1681.

[31] Local Government Act 1972, Sections 123 and 127.

9

Closed Churchyards, Churchyards Affected by Redundancy and Inner City Churchyards

As has been noted in chapter 5, on churchyards and the general law, the land surrounding a consecrated church, whether or not it is consecrated, and also detached consecrated burial grounds, are subject to the jurisdiction of the Bishop, exercised by the Diocesan Chancellor in the Consistory Court. In general, no alterations may be made without the sanction of a faculty from the Court. The Pastoral Measure 1983 and certain other legislation contain powers which cut across this general provision.

CLOSURE OF CHURCHYARDS

Burial grounds may be closed for burials, wholly or subject to exceptions, by Order in Council made under statutory authority, and many churchyards have been closed in this way.

No bodies may be buried in contravention of an Order in Council but the prohibition does not extend to cremated remains, which, as we have seen in chapter 6, may still be interred in a closed churchyard pursuant to a faculty. Apart from this limitation on burials, all legal rights and liabilities and the jurisdiction of the Consistory Court remain unaffected, save in the important respect discussed in chapter 8, of which PCCs could more often take advantage, namely when the local authority has been called on to accept responsibility for the maintenance of the churchyard.

If a question arises as to whether a particular burial ground has been formally closed, it may be necessary to ascertain whether an Order in Council has been made. If no copy can be found amongst the parochial records, in the records of the Diocesan Registrar or in the local Records Office, the indices of the London Gazette should be traced for references prior to 1891 and thereafter the indices of the annual volumes of the Statutory Rules and Orders. This may be a lengthy exercise. Enquiries may also be made of the Department of the Environment.

If an incumbent and PCC wish a churchyard to be closed, so that responsibility for maintenance may be transferred to the local authority or so as to terminate the incumbents's responsibility for providing future burial space, approach should be made to the Church of England Churchyards section of the Department of the Environment, giving details of the churchyard concerned, with the reasons for seeking an Order, and asking for steps to be taken to obtain an Order in Council under the Burial Act 1853.[1]

In practice the Department will support an application (a) if the continuing use of the churchyard for burials could constitute a risk to public health, or (b) would be contrary to decency; (c) if the discontinuance of burials would prevent or mitigate a nuisance; or (d) if the churchyard is full. A desire on the part of the parish to be relieved of the responsibility or maintenance would not be sufficient to obtain an Order, and an application will not normally be considered if it relates only to part of the churchyard. When asked to obtain an Order the Department of the Environment will carry out consultations with the relevant local authorities and will provide the applicants with details as to how the application should be publicised in the local press.

DISUSED CHURCH GROUNDS

A burial ground closed by Order in Council (whether or not subject to exceptions) is a disused burial ground, and under the Disused Burial Grounds Act 1884, there is a statutory prohibition against building on disused burial grounds generally.[2] This prohibition is not applicable in respect of the curtilage of a church where burials have never occurred, although a faculty and secular planning consent will be required for any building on such land. Also, the prohibition does not apply where a burial ground is used to enlarge the church, for which purpose a faculty may still be granted. The Pastoral Measure 1983 provides for further cases where building may take place in a churchyard where there have been burials, either by a Pastoral Scheme or by a Redundancy Scheme.

PASTORAL SCHEMES

The Church Commissioners are empowered by Section 30 of the Pastoral Measure 1983 to make Pastoral Schemes which may provide for the appropriation, to such use or uses specified in the scheme, (a) of the whole or any part of a churchyard or other land annexed or belonging to a church, (b) any burial ground vested in the incumbent or a benefice which is not annexed to a church, or (c) any other burial ground which is subject to the jurisdiction of the Bishop. The scheme may provide for the disposal of the land for specified uses or without such restriction. This power has been used to allow, for example, the erection of a parsonage house or parish hall within a churchyard and for its transfer, freed from the legal effects of consecration, to the incumbent or parochial church council, as the case may be. Where a churchyard affected by such a pastoral scheme has been used for burial and contains tombstones, the provisions of Section 65 and Schedule 6 of the Measure for dealing with them will apply. These are discussed in more detail below.

As explained in chapter 7, under the Open Spaces Act 1906, there is provision whereby a disused burial ground may be transferred to the local authority, for value or otherwise, for use as an open space.[3] A faculty is still required before the local authority may make alterations or exercise powers of management over such a churchyard but, subject to the terms of the faculty, tombstones may be removed and the ground laid out afresh. The open space thus acquired may, if the faculty so permits, be used for games. For example, tennis courts have been made on the old churchyard of St Botolph, Bishopsgate, in the City of London.

CHURCHYARDS BELONGING TO REDUNDANT CHURCHES

The Church Commissioners have power under Section 28 of the Pastoral Measure 1983, to make a Pastoral Scheme providing for a declaration of redundancy in respect of a consecrated church building. This may be to allow for a modern church building or because no church is needed any longer on the site. Provision may be made under Section 46 for replacement by a new building, or by Section 47 for the original building to be put to a suitable new use.[4] If such a scheme does not specifically deal with the churchyard it remains vested in the incumbent and subject to faculty jurisdiction in the usual way, although it may be affected by subsequent proceedings under the Measure.

When a church has been declared redundant by a Pastoral Scheme, within a period of three years from the date of redundancy, the commissioners must prepare a further scheme, called a Redundancy Scheme, providing for the future of the building.[5] Under Section 51, the Measure provides four alternatives for the building's future, namely:

1 Appropriation to a suitable alternative use;
2 Preservation by the Redundant Churches Fund;
3 Vesting in the Diocesan Board of Finance on specified terms;
4 Demolition.

The Commissioners are empowered, when preparing a Redundancy Scheme (or a Pastoral Scheme under the special provisions of Sections 46 and 47 of the Measure), to include provisions dealing with the whole or a part of the churchyard annexed to the redundant church, whether or not it has been consecrated and used for burial.

If the church building is to be put to a suitable alternative use, or if it is to be demolished and the site used for a new purpose, then the churchyard or a part of it may be used for the same or an ancillary purpose. Under the Scheme, the land and buildings may be disposed of by the Commissioners, together or separately, by sale, gift or exchange; or they may be leased by the Diocesan Board of Finance. Frequently only the building itself is put to an alternative use; but in such a case it is usually necessary to provide in the Scheme for a right of way over the churchyard, so as to give access to the redundant church to its new owner and allow for a right of access to the part of the churchyard which surrounds the building for the purpose of carrying out repairs.

Where a Scheme provides for a redundant church to be vested in the Redundant Churches Fund or in the Diocesan Board of Finance for care and maintenance, the churchyard may be vested in the Fund as well. However, this is not mandatory and it may be inappropriate, especially if burials are to be continued. Here again, a right of way for access and a right of access for repairs would be provided for in the Scheme.

The Commissioners must publish all Pastoral and Redundancy Schemes as drafts and must consider any representations about the draft before making the Scheme and submitting it for confirmation to Her Majesty in Council.[6]

BURIALS, HUMAN REMAINS AND MONUMENTS

When a Redundancy Scheme becomes effective, unless the scheme provides otherwise, a redundant church and churchyard affected by the Scheme cease to be subject to the legal effects of consecration and to faculty jurisdiction.[7] The exception to this is where a redundant church, and perhaps the churchyard also, is vested in the Redundant Churches Fund. In this case the legal effects of consecration continue to apply, but faculty jurisdiction ceases and the incumbent, churchwardens and PCC cease to have any special rights, unless the church is restored to use, as is possible under the Pastoral Measure. In that case the church will again vest in the incumbent, and so may the churchyard. Unless and until this occurs, burials may only take place on express request to the Fund and will only be permitted in exceptional cases. Where a churchyard is vested in the Fund, this is usually so as to preserve the aesthetic impact of the church. Proposed memorials are subject to strict scrutiny.

Although the Disused Burial Grounds Act 1884 prohibits the erection of buildings upon disused burial grounds,[8] the Pastoral Measure 1983 removes this prohibition in relation to Pastoral and Redundancy Schemes respectively, provided (a) that no person has been buried during the fifty years immediately before the making of the scheme in the churchyard to which it relates, or (b) that, if burials have taken place within fifty years, no relative or personal representative of the deceased person has sustained an objection to the scheme.[9]

Where a Redundancy or Pastoral Scheme provides for the disposal of a churchyard which has been used for burial, it vests in either the Church Commissioners or the Diocesan Board of Finance, freed from burial rights. But the Measure makes provision for the payment of compensation for the loss of these rights.[10]

If a churchyard or burial ground which has been used for burials and contains tombstones is to be put to another use by a Redundancy Scheme or a Pastoral Scheme, there are special provisions under Section 65 and Schedule 6 of the Measure about the disposal of human remains and tombstones that must be complied with. A notice must be published setting out the proposals for dealing with remains and tombstones (in some circumstances a copy being served upon next of kin or personal representatives of the deceased person) and attention must be drawn to the right of relatives or, in relevant cases, the Commonwealth War Graves Commission, to undertake the removal of remains and the disposal of tombstones themselves in a manner other than that set out in the notice.

Generally, all human remains must be removed and re-interred or cremated, and all tombstones, monuments and memorials must be disposed of before demolishing, selling, leasing, or otherwise disposing of the property. However, this provision does not apply when a church is entrusted to the Redundant Churches Fund;[11] nor does it apply where the redundant church is to be used, without structural change, as a place of worship by a university, college, school or other institution, or as a private chapel or monument, or for worship by a Church other than the Church of England.[12] In other cases the Home Secretary may make an Order, under Section 65 (3) of the Measure, dispensing with this requirement so far as human remains are concerned, if he is satisfied that the intended use or development of the property would not involve the disturbance of human remains. There is no provision in the Measure for a similar 'dispensing order' in respect of the requirement of Section 65 (1) to dispose of tombstones, monuments and memorials commemorating deceased persons interred in the churchyard.

Monuments and memorials commemorating deceased persons buried elsewhere than in the property affected by the Redundancy Scheme are disposed of in such a manner as the Bishop, after consulting the Diocesan Advisory Committee, shall direct.[14] Disposal in this way is often in practice taken to include a direction, in suitable cases, to leave them *in situ* in the church or churchyard, although in cases where a church is to be demolished monuments from it must be disposed of by removal elsewhere or, failing that, by being broken up and defaced.

As to tombstones, monuments and memorials commemorating persons interred in the property which is the subject of the Redundancy Scheme, where it is proposed to remove the human remains to which they relate and re-inter them elsewhere, the Measure contemplates where reasonably practicable the removal of the tombstones, monuments or memorials and setting them up in the new place of interment or other suitable place.[15]

Whether or not human remains are to be moved, in cases where it is not appropriate to remove and re-site memorials, these will normally be left *in situ,* provided this is both practicable and fitting.[16] Otherwise they are offered by the landowner, usually the Church Commissioners or the Diocesan Board of Finance, to the Bishop for preservation. He is required to consult the Diocesan Advisory Committee about the disposal of a tombstone, monument or memorial and if, following this, they are not accepted by the Bishop for preservation, they are required to be broken and defaced before being otherwise disposed of. This is appropriate where a tombstone is so worn that no inscription recording the name of the deceased survives. Brass plates which have no intrinsic or historic interest may be buried after the inscriptions have been recorded and photographs taken.

If the tombstones remain *in situ,* the churchyard will pass into hands other than those of the Church, as will the ownership of the tombstones, and there may be difficulties of access for the general public unless the conveyance by the Church Commissioners or the lease by the Diocesan Board of Finance make provision for such access. Where a grave is being tended regularly or some well-known person is buried, limited access is normally imposed in the conveyance or lease. Where the tombstones are not to remain *in situ*, but are of such merit that the Bishop accepts them for preservation, the difficulty is likely to be that of finding somewhere else to re-erect them, especially if the human remains are not also to be removed.

When tombstones or other materials are removed from the churchyard, the landowner must within two months from the date of removal deposit with the council of the district (or London borough) concerned a record of the removal, with sufficient particulars to identify the memorial (including a copy of any inscription on it) and show the date and manner of its removal and disposal, and the place (if any) to which it is transferred. A copy of this record must also be deposited with the Registrar General of Births, Deaths and Marriages.[17] In considering the course of action to adopt in dealing with unwanted memorials where a churchyard is closed or subject to a scheme, it may be helpful to consider the practice of the Chancellor with respect to analogous situations where the churchyard is in use, as discussed in chapter 6.

THE INNER CITY CHURCHYARD

The inner city churchyard may be of particular value to the community even though today it will often not be used for burials. The legal responsibility for maintaining it and keeping it safe applies as much as anywhere else. So, too, do secular planning controls. Some legislation may be particularly useful, such as that for controlling litter.

The resources or inner city churches are greatly stretched, and maintaining a churchyard may seem an unnecessary expense. If the churchyard is full it may be particularly desirable for it to be formally closed by Order in Council, as discussed earlier in this chapter, and transferred to the local authority, under the powers looked at in chapter 8, so that it may be looked after and used as a public open space. This will relieve the church of the expense and of responsibility for protecting the public using the churchyard from harm. It may also enable a more attractive and open setting to be provided for the church, which will enhance its witness to the community. In the rare case of a churchyard in a run-down urban area not being full, it is likely that the Department of the Environment will support an application for an Order in Council to close it on grounds of protecting public decency.

Especially if an inner city churchyard is small, or if the church has only a narrow curtilage of ground around it which may never have been used for burials, it may be particularly important for it to be retained in the ownership of the church. In such circumstances the local authority may still be prepared to take over control and maintenance under the Open Spaces Act 1906. Also the various other ways that local authorities may help, and which are reviewed in chapter 8, may be particularly useful.

If a church is in an area designated under the Inner Urban Areas Act 1978, it may be possible for a re-ordering scheme to be made for part or for the whole of the surroundings of the church in partnership with the local authority. If the local authority agrees on such a scheme it must be approved by the Department of the Environment, since the greater part of the money will be provided by central government. Such schemes can provide for construction of fencing and walls, landscaping with planting of trees, shrubs and other plants, and the restoration of any structure in the churchyard.[18]

In an area prone to vandalism and misbehaviour it may be in the public interest for the area around a church to be open and for there to be no new burials. However, if there are any tombstones in the churchyard it may be important to ensure that at least the best of them are preserved, so as to retain the character of a churchyard. All statutory requirements and the need for a faculty where this is still necessary must be carefully borne in mind. The arrangements for public help in the inner city are subject to frequent change. It is important for inner city churches to keep in contact with the planning and other appropriate departments of their district council to see what new opportunities arise where the church can take a lead in the revival of their area, not least in restoring church buildings and their surroundings as a focus for community life and spiritual witness.

NOTES

[1] Burial Act 1853, as amended by Local Government Act 1972, Section 214, and Schedule 26, paragraph 15. This amendment extends the power to make Closing Orders to all burial grounds in Greater London and to all local authority burial grounds throughout the country. Most churchyards were covered by the original Act, but there may be certain church burial grounds where there is no power to make a Closing Order: that is where the burial ground was itself set up under a particular Act of Parliament or under a central government Order. See generally here Department of the Environment 'Notes on Orders requiring the discontinuance of burials in Church of England Church Yards'. Note BC3 (R).

[2] Disused Burial Grounds Act 1884, Section 3.

[3] Open Spaces Act 1906, Section 9(a).

[4] Pastoral Measure 1983, Section 47(i)

[5] *Ibid*, cf Sections 47(2) and (3). See generally Sections 48-54.

[6] *Ibid*, Sections 3-1.

[7] *Ibid*, Section 61.

[8] *Supra*, note 2.

[9] Pastoral Measure 1983, Sections 30(4) and 51(11).

[10] *Ibid*, Section 59(7).

[11] *Ibid*, Section 65(1).

[12] *Ibid*, Section 65(2).

[13] *Ibid*, Section 65(3).

[14] *Ibid*, Schedule 6, paragraphs 6 and 9.

[15] *Ibid*, Schedule 6, paragraphs 3-5.

[16] *Ibid*, Schedule 6, paragraph 6.

[17] *Ibid*, Schedule 6 paragraph 10 and see 7.

[18] Inner Urban Areas Act 1978, section 5.

Part III
Practical Considerations

Commissioning a New Memorial

In the twelve years that have elapsed since the previous edition of the *Churchyards Handbook* there have been many changes in Church and Society, and therefore many changes in emphasis when it comes to the giving of advice about the commissioning of new monuments in churchyards (or, for that matter, churches) and here are some of them:

(i) Whereas ten years ago death was the 'great unmentionable', there has recently been a renewed openness to the experience of death, and a rich literature has been published – most notably, the publication in 1981 of a good English translation of Philippe Aries's remarkable study of death and commemoration, *The Hour of Our Death* (Paris, 1977). At the same time much thought is currently given to the counselling of the bereaved; people are specially trained for this work, both priests and laity, and a specialist literature is developing. At the same time, some people have a natural gift for counselling and a special empathy for the dying and the bereaved. This whole area of discussion is crucial to the study of monuments, and to the commissioning of monuments; on the one hand there is evidence to suggest that the immediate commissioning of a tombstone may be a too obvious way of assuaging grief, or even of expiating a sense of guilt (and which of us has nothing to regret at the loss of a friend or relative?) and, on the other hand, the more thoughtful commissioning of a tombstone may be part of the amortizing process of bereavement, in which the careful choice of a really apposite epitaph or inscription, and the evolution of a design through trust in an appropriate artist or craftsman, may be part of the process of reconciliation and acceptance of death. Above all, the commissioning of a tombstone must be something personal.

(ii) So far as taste is concerned there has been a growing feeling that we have not been getting the tombstones and other memorials which, as a society of caring human beings, we need and deserve. The mass-produced product has begun – and not before time – to provoke a strong reaction. Responsible monumental masons, both individually and corporately, have been quick to respond to the new challenge; and, in addition, there are literally dozens of young letter-cutters and sculptors, graduates of colleges of art, who are eager to see tombstones as a normal healthy staple part of their repertoire and work, and who are willing to work closely and sensitively with clients to produce headstones or other forms of memorial (for example, wall plaques recording the interment of cremated remains).

(iii) The number of cremations, as opposed to burials or inhumations, has continued to grow, and this has in its turn stimulated both thought and experiment in relation to the commemoration of cremated remains. More is said on this subject below.

(iv) The past decade has seen an immense growth in informed public concern about conservation, in all its aspects. So far as churchyards are concerned this has had, and is having, a number of significant implications:

(a) churchyards and their memorials are being more studied and recorded than at any previous time in their history, and this is also stimulating the growth of a specialist literature;

(b) churchyards are being increasingly appreciated as habitats of wildlife, both flora and fauna, and this aspect of churchyards has produced television and radio programmes, countless articles, and nationwide activity on the part of county naturalists' trusts;

(c) tombstones up to the mid-nineteenth century are being systematically 'listed as being of special architectural or historic interest' by the Historic Buildings and Monuments Commiss-

Plate 22. *Alec Peever's flowing lettering responds sympathetically to the acute sense of loss felt at the death of a small child.*

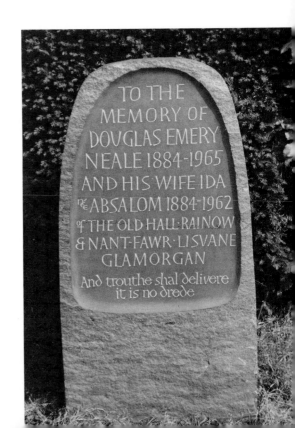

Plate 23. *Rainow, Cheshire: John Skelton's headstones are infinitely inventive (see also the back cover).*

Plate 24.   *Imogen Holst, a greatly loved figure in Aldeburgh, Suffolk is there commemorated by this headstone designed and made by Martin Jennings.*

Plate 25.   *The central cross in the churchyard extension at Penn, Buckinghamshire is a fine focal work of art by local sculptor, Darsie Rawlins.*

Plate 26. *Sutton, Cambridgeshire: in this subtle variation on the traditional headstone shape Tom Perkins achieves a quiet distinction.*

Plate 27. *Owlpen, Gloucestershire: Bryant Fedden wittily commemorates a bee-keeper.*

Plate 28. *Sarah More is one of many excellent sculptors and letter-cutters who have trained at the City and Guilds of London Art School in Kennington.*

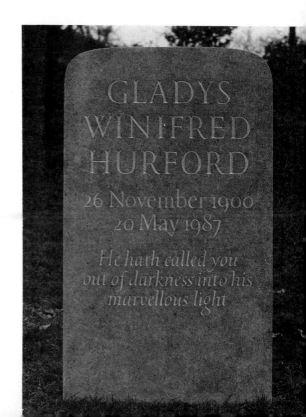

FRANCIS
JACKSON
1897 1985

FOR THEY
SHALL SEE
GOD

GLADYS
WINIFRED
HURFORD

26 November 1900
20 May 1987

*He hath called you
out of darkness into his
marvellous light*

Plate 29. *Minehead Cemetery: a recent good headstone by Caroline Webb, executed in Purbeck stone.*

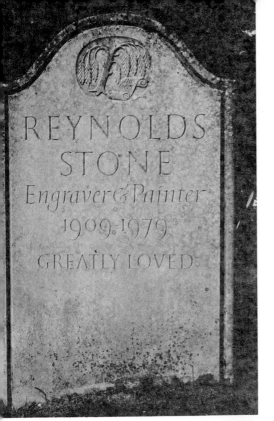

Plate 30. *Litton Cheney, Dorset: Michael Harvey has fittingly commemorated Reynolds Stone, one of the finest engravers and letterers of our time.*

Plate 31. *Note the flourish in the last letter of 'Huxley' in this memorial by Richard Kindersley.*

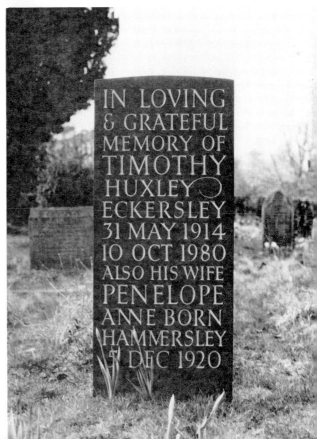

Plate 32.   *If a small flat stone is used to mark the burying place of cremated remains, then this example by Richard Kindersley provides an admirable model.*

Plate 33.   *By using contrasting letter forms Nicholas Sloan's headstone achieves a striking artistic effect.*

In
loving memory of
MALCOLM TARLTON
who died on
the 10th January 1986
aged 54 years
husband father brother friend

Plate 34. *Chevington, Gloucestershire: well-conceived Classical Revival by local sculptor, Rory Young.*

Plate 35. *Arncliffe, North Yorkshire: appropriately rugged memorial to Bishop John Robinson, by John Shaw.*

Plate 36. *Histon, Cambridgeshire: a headstone by David Kindersley, one of the really outstanding practitioners of this art.*

ion for England on behalf of the Secretary of State for the Environment;

(d) in the case of a listed church (and more than 12,000 Church of England churches *are* listed) or in the case of churches in Conservation Areas, there is less and less tolerance – fortunately, we may say – of the visually brutal and inept when it comes to the introduction of new memorials or unsuitable materials.

What is suitable, it is then sensible to ask. And how should the conscientious parish, through its incumbent and PCC, go about encouraging good design in churchyard memorials? What is the equally conscientious mourner to do? And who will help him to do it?

WHAT IS SUITABLE DEPENDS LARGELY ON THE CONTEXT

It must, surely, be obvious that in a churchyard in which the focus is the parish church – generally of mellow stone, or maybe (if eighteenth- or nineteenth-century) of brick – the choice of material must be sympathetic to the *genius loci*. The place of origin is not so important as is congruity. However, Italian marble is inappropriate not because it is Italian but because it will look alien (marble not being a normal building material in English climatic conditions); and a French or German limestone or sandstone may well be very appropriate if it is similar to or sympathetic to the surrounding historic materials in colour and texture.

The next question is scale. The proliferation of many diminutive headstones to commemorate the interment of cremated remains is an obvious example. Against the scale of the church building and of older and larger stones, these stones all too readily convey an impression of a pets' cemetery, and the effect is risible or distasteful instead of being dignified and consoling. Again the solution will depend on context. At Penn in Buckinghamshire, a large but scattered country village, cremated remains are buried beneath stone slabs – not too large in size – bordering the main paths in the churchyard extension. On these flat stones names and dates, and perhaps a short epitaph (over which much care is taken), are inscribed. In twenty years' time, or more, the stones can be turned over and re-used. The need for commemoration rarely exists beyond one generation and, in any case, even where there are inscribed stones there should always exist a handsome book in which names can be inscribed. In a churchyard where there are many such interments, it may indeed be prudent to take a wise and early policy of disallowing individual commemoration in the churchyard; the proper development of a Book of Remembrance can be an artistic opportunity in its own right, and whether it is acceptable practically and emotionally to the bereaved will depend on the seriousness and reverence with which the project is undertaken, and the way in which the Book is displayed and made accessible. By contrast, in a churchyard where only one or two such interments are made each year it may serve well to have a single large inscribed plaque, with a well-chosen epitaph, and then for names and dates to be inscribed upon it as they occur.

HOW SHOULD A CONSCIENTIOUS PARISH ENCOURAGE GOOD DESIGN?

First of all by talking through and evolving a policy which is right for that place, having taken as much disinterested *outside* advice as possible.

Advice should be sought, as to the availability and appropriateness of craftsmen, from the Diocesan Advisory Committee for the Care of Churches, the CCC, and the regional arts councils, and the Crafts Council at national level.

Again the example of Penn may be useful. In the churchyard extension (enclosed by partly eighteenth-century set-brick walls) the central sculpture – a churchyard cross, in effect, with a Crucifixion carved on one side and the comforting image of Mary and the Christ Child on the other – and many of the headstones use the work of a sculptor who lives in the parish, a senior member of the Art Workers Guild. Bereaved parishioners are not *obliged* to employ him, nor would this be right if it was a regulation; but other stones are required to bear a 'family resemblance', and this has had the result that the two or three good monumental masons in the neighbourhood strive very hard to equal, or even exceed, the standard which has been set for them.

Parishes should not hesitate to set and maintain very firm regulations; but they must ensure that these are available in written form and very widely known in the parish, and helpful to undertakers and monumental masons in the wider neighbourhood.

Parishes should not hesitate to require high artistic standards. In tombstone design, as in much else, there is no or little financial disadvantage in preferring the meretricious to the good and enduring. Often, in fact, the balance of advantage lies the other way.

WHAT SHOULD A CONSCIENTIOUS MOURNER DO?

What he or she should *not* do is to place an order or commission a memorial in any form without consultation and without permission.

In the first place a chief mourner should be handed, at the time of the funeral, a clear and kindly memorandum setting out the considerations which apply: that the churchyard is public, not a private place, and all that is erected in it must show good manners in its context and to its neighbourhood; that its maintenance is a common responsibility, and should not be made more difficult by e.g. curbstones; that it is the setting for a living place of worship, and beauty and harmony and grace are important attributes for a churchyard. The memorandum should go on to specify any detailed requirements, and suggest discussion wih incumbent or churchwarden about the choice of sculptor or mason. Wide sources of advice should be indicated, and *specified* with addresses. The availability of a form for authorisation should also be indicated.

WHO WILL HELP?

For someone who *really* wants to take trouble over choosing a craftsman to make a good headstone the best sources would be the Crafts Council (who produce an excellent list of letter-cutters and calligraphers, with addresses) and the CCC, which has an extensive Register of Artists and Craftsmen. At county or diocesan level the equivalents should be the regional arts association, the county guild of artists and craftsmen, and the DAC.

11

Stones for New Memorials

It is important that the stones recommended for memorials in churchyards should be those which harmonise with their surroundings and are of durable quality. However, it is not possible to be specific about which particular stones will have a pleasing effect and harmonise in any given area. In making a choice local experience is an invaluable guide, and advice may be sought from a Regional Office of the National Association of Master Masons, whose name and address may be obtained from their Head Office at Crown Buildings, High Street, Aylesbury, Buckinghamshire HP20 1SL. The *Natural Stone Directory*, 6th Edition, 1985 (Ealing Publications Ltd, Weir Bank, Bray, Maidenhead, Berkshire SL6 2ED) is also a source of useful information. Availability of stone of monumental quality can change from time to time, and up-to-date information should be obtained before any particular stone is specifically recommended.

The 'monumental' quality stone referred to in this chapter, is that which has been selected specially by the quarrier, and put aside for the purpose. It should be of reasonable size, without flaws, marks and blemishes, which are not noticeable on a building, bridge or public works structure, but which are not acceptable on the surface being used for a memorial which is more likely to be critically examined.

British stones which at present are not only suitable but readily available on a national basis are Portland, York and the Devon and Cornish granites. Foreign stones may be acceptable as substitutes for indigenous stones which have previously been used in a diocese or parish, but which are no longer available in monumental quality, the main criterion in this instance being that the stone is in harmony with its surroundings. If there is any doubt over the inclusion of any particular stone on a list of stones acceptable within a diocese, a sample should be requested from the local masons. It is important that a stone should not be discriminated against solely on the basis of its country of origin, particularly where the country of origin is within the EEC.

The following list of stones has been prepared in consultation with geologists, monumental masons and architects. It makes no claim to be exhaustive and is intended to be used only as a guide, but it includes a sufficient variety of stones to provide an example of those which may be found to be satisfactory in churchyards.

BRITISH STONES

Limestones

The limestones of Jurassic age of Dorset and the adjoining counties, and the carboniferous limestone of Derbyshire and Cumbria have been found to be particularly suitable. The oolitic limestones of Leicestershire and Oxfordshire have been found suitable in some instances, but can only be recommended with circumspection in areas subject to high pollution.

Sandstone

Most of the fine grained sandstones from Yorkshire (carboniferous: coal measures and millstone grit) are available in a variety of shades of brown and blue-grey. Sandstone of monumental quality is also available from Cheshire, Cumbria and Derbyshire in shades varying from pinkish to yellowish-brown. Co. Durham and Northumberland have light bluish-grey and purplish-grey sandstones of suitable quality. Gloucestershire and South Wales provide Pennant sandstone in a variety of grey, greyish-blue and green.

Slate

Cumbria, Cornwall and North Wales can all provide suitable slate in varying shades of green, grey and blue. All slates are capable of taking fine lettering, but not all are suitable for use in polluted atmospheres or in salt-contaminated soils.

Granite

The granite masses of Cornwall and Devon produce the best known British granites. They are generally medium-to-light grey. The granite of Cumbria and some of the granites again being quarried in Scotland may also be considered suitable.

FOREIGN STONES

Britain does not produce a large number of stones which are readily available and of monumental quality. Foreign stones of appropriate colour and texture for the context in which the material will be placed, may therefore provide a suitable alternative. The beautiful and durable limestones of Northern Italy, some of the French limestones (recently used for cathedral restoration in England) and certain Portuguese stones may be worthy of consideration. Granite from Italy and France, and other imported granites, traditionally used by the Scottish granite industry, are consistent in quality and readily available.

In the environs of a stone-built church of historic and architectural distinction, it is necessary to maintain the character of the church. Local building stone may not be currently of a suitable quality, but it is reasonable to expect that the stone used for memorials should be of a similar shade and texture to those of the church. In an urban area where the church is not built of stone, or in a churchyard extension where the burial ground is well screened from the church, there may be instances where a greater variety of stone is not out of place, and indeed may add interest to an otherwise dull area. As is said elsewhere in this Handbook, the question of appropriateness of context is all-important in deciding what material to use in a particular situation.

12

Epitaphs and Inscriptions

Epitaphs are an ancient literary form. The best are both moving and delightful, because strong feeling or serious intent have in them found perfect expression. It is a matter of style, and the composer of an epitaph must not only know exactly what he wants to say but how to say it as concisely as possible. The longest epitaph is short compared with a newspaper obituary, so it cannot afford to contain any but essential words. Mourners should never be encouraged to lengthen an inscription into vapidity with pious sentiments, merely for the look of the thing, or for a fancied seemliness. Every word must tell, and will only do so if it is necessary and sincere. Equally, mourners should not be required to say less than they want to. It is as hard to say in principle what is the proper length for an epitaph as what is the proper length of a piece of string. These considerations ought to be borne in mind, even when the epitaph to be composed will, like the vast majority, do little more than record a name and two dates.

The objects of a modern epitaph will usually be some or all of the following: to identify the resting place of the mortal remains of a dead person; to honour the dead; to comfort the living; to inform posterity. In the past two other objects have occurred: to edify the reader, usually by reminders of the inevitability of death and judgment; and to boast of the wealth, breeding or lofty family connexions of the dead. Nowadays we lack the self-confidence to carve a sermon, however brief, on a tombstone; and, it is to be hoped, no longer care to immortalise our snobbery. The other four objects are legitimate enough. In sanctioning them an incumbent cannot offend conscience. He must hope that his influence will protect the dead and the mourners alike from faults of taste, but canons of taste cannot be made as strict as the rules of grammar. The wise priest will, when in doubt, err on the side of charity, for epitaphs are expressions of love, and as such even some of the silliest may be respected. Accordingly it should very seldom be necessary to forbid an inscription outright, and it is reassuring to know that even then mourners can apply to the Consistory Court for a faculty, if they do not accept the incumbent's ruling or that of the Diocesan Advisory Committee.

In the present century the art of writing epitaphs has almost wholly died out in England. This is partly because of the rise in the cost of inscriptions, but chiefly because of a morbid desire to avoid the excesses of the past, when epitaphs were too often wordy and insincere. As a result, our burial grounds are becoming deserts of verbal, as well as visual, banality. This can be to no-one's advantage. Not for nothing is one of the best-loved poems in the language entitled 'Elegy in a Country Churchyard'. The consecrated ground of a churchyard, like a church itself, should be a reverenced place, where everything should, as much as possible, enrich the spirit. In this process epitaphs have their part to play.

Practicalities first. A certain minimum of information is necessary. Full name, without abbreviation: 'John William Brown', not simply 'John Brown' or 'J. W. Brown'. He must not be confused with others of like names. When the inscription relates to more than one person it should read '. . . and Mary Jane, his wife', or 'Mary Jane, his wife, and Jane Anna, their daughter', to avoid repeating the surname. If the wife dies first, it should read 'Mary Jane, wife of John William Brown'; if the husband, 'John William, husband of Mary Jane Brown'. However, if the survivor is likely to be commemorated later on the same tombstone it should read 'Mary Jane Brown (dates)'. In the case of a wife who has chosen not to adopt her husband's surname – which will probably become more and more usual – the form should be 'Mary Jane Green, wife of John William Brown'. Dates of birth and death should be put in the most unambiguous form possible: 'Born 21 May 1901, died 7 July 1978' is absolutely safe, in a way that variants 'Died July 8, 1978, aged 77 years' are not.

Roman numerals (MCMLXXVIII) may be troublesome to decipher, but are much more beautiful than Arabic numerals on inscriptions.

A few other points must command general agreement. Advise against expressions such as 'fell asleep' for 'died' unless they make a special point, like the Salvation Army officer who, said his epitaph, was 'promoted to glory'. It is absurd, in a churchyard of all places, to shrink away from the fact of death. An epitaph is a public document, and not a cosy one at that. Nicknames or pet-names ('Mum', 'Dad', 'Ginger') inscribed in stone, would carry overtones of the dog-cemetery unsuitable for the resting place of Christian men and women. When a biblical text is used it is quite superfluous to give the reference. 'Until the day dawn (2 Pet. i. 19)' is not only unnecessary, and therefore inelegant: it distracts attention from the message to the form of what is said. The Psalms should be quoted from the Book of Common Prayer, as the most familiar version, or some may prefer the revised Psalter; all other biblical texts should surely come from the Authorised Version, the most splendid well of language at our disposal. But it is not necessary to confine choice to the Bible. Felicitous quotations from the Prayer Book, hymns or secular sources, poetry, or prose, are wholly acceptable, so long as they are truly felicitous and (in the case of the latter) consistent with Christian belief. To make sure that they are it is always prudent to check their context.

Mourners must supply the mason with a transcript of the exact wording, lettering and punctuation which they require, and impress on him that it is not to be departed from without the incumbent's authority. On the form of lettering, and the arrangement of the composition as a whole, the advice of the mason should be sought. Lettering should be uniform in style – e.g. not partly Roman and partly Old English; though it need not be uniform in size, and capitals, lower case and italics may be mixed, provided they are all of the same style or 'fount', as printers call it. The wise incumbent will acquire some knowledge of the aesthetics of typography, since notably well-arranged and lettered inscriptions add much to a churchyard. The name may with advantage be larger than the rest of the text. To preserve legibility, lettering may have two coats of paint, the second coat not black but a shade darker or lighter than the stone.

If observed in the proper spirit, these principles will put those concerned on the fair road to composing a decent epitaph. But they may be ambitious to do more. If so, they must rely chiefly on their own sense of what is fitting and right. An experienced priest will have good advice to give, and, even more important, will know how to offer it acceptably. What follows is only a suggestion of what should be borne in mind.

HONOUR THE DEAD

Nowadays an epitaph need not, therefore should not, aim at the completeness of an adequate obituary. The particulars of any notable career will be better preserved in the back numbers of the Press, whether national or local, or in the countless records that society today amasses. A maker of epitaphs should seek chiefly to evoke the salient points of a man's character, only those achievements and honours which bring that character to life needing to be mentioned. This can be done in various ways. For example, when Lord and Lady Glenconner wanted to commemorate their son Edward, who was killed in the battle of the Somme, they quoted from an eye-witness account of his conduct in battle: 'When things were at their worst he would go up and down in the trenches cheering the men, when danger was greatest his smile was loveliest.' This carries much greater conviction than a more timid and conventional way of recording the young man's gallantry could have. On the other hand, sometimes the plainest statements ring truest, as with John Cook of Sutton, Cambs., who died aged 74 years having been, we are assured, 'many Years a respectable Collar and Harness maker of this Parish'. This is much better than the condescending assurance that John Parr 'was ranger of Dunham Park, under the NOBLE EARL of Stamford and Warrington, for thirty-three years, which Situation he filled with credit to himself and Satisfaction to his Noble employer'. But it is easy to believe, of all three men, that they did their duty in their generation.

Boasting and snobbery being unseemly, it is best to omit all official honours and distinctions save the very highest, which it would be both misleading and mock-modest to leave out. Titles which form part of a man's name, like a knighthood or a peerage, should normally be included, on the same principle which suggests the advisability of including a man's trade: it makes him easier to identify. Edward Elgar's tomb tells us simply and sufficiently that he had the Order of Merit and was Master of the King's Musick. With equal dignity William Peach of Repton is identified as the village blacksmith.

When the titles and professions are included it is important to get them right. The proper form for a clergyman is 'John Smith, Priest' (the acceptable alternative, 'Clerk in Holy Orders', is perhaps a little precious). Dignitaries and grandees may be treated quite as economically: 'James, Earl of Radburne', not 'The Right Honourable James', etc (but 'Sir Julian Long, Baronet', not 'Julian Long, Baronet'). Common qualifications such as MA, FRICS and the like should rarely appear in an epitaph. The rule to observe, as always, is economy. Nothing immaterial should appear on a tombstone.

COMFORT THE LIVING

This is surely the most deeply-felt purpose of epitaphs – hence the innumerable affirmations that the dead are safe in heaven, the proclamations of loving grief: hence indeed the whole impulse to tend graves and to honour the memories of the departed with tombstones and inscriptions. A Church which has given the world the infinitely consoling Order for the Burial of the Dead cannot, in charity, be too restrictive in the advice it gives to mourners who wish to discharge their feelings in epitaphs. Indeed it probably ought to encourage them. Tombstones weather so quickly that they cannot, in the eye of eternity, seem appreciably more durable than paper or wood; and among the epitaphs that survive from the greatest age of English inscriptions, the seventeenth century, are many which still ring true – which still, in the richest sense of the word, endure – precisely because they were unselfconscious outpourings of deep feeling:

> . . . I'll visit thee, and when I leave this light
> Come spend my days in the same cell of night
> Where thou art lodged, and Love shall Death enforce
> To recompense the wrong of our divorce.   (St Mary's, Stafford)

This, from a husband to a wife, was the best honour that could be paid her, and the best possible comfort to the husband, and makes, in every way, the best reading for posterity. The twentieth century cannot reasonably hope to be so eloquent, but there is no cause for it to be tongue-tied.

True, there are dangers. The wise incumbent will wish to protect mourners and dead alike from solecisms; and he may see his way to discourage the use of cliché. The Authorised Version alone is so full of appropriate matter that it is depressing, and ultimately unconvincing, to come across the same half-dozen texts again and again. The same holds true of stock phrases such as 'the dearly loved wife'. Sincerity cannot well convey itself through worn-out language. But this point should not guide conduct too strictly. Nothing could be more unfortunate than wrangling over matters of taste, at the very graveside, when the purpose of the enterprise is consolation. If mourners insist on clichés, they must have them.

INFORM POSTERITY

To a great extent this object has been covered by what has been said of the others, but it deserves a few further words. In the past the oddest things have been recorded on tombstones (probably because that was the only way they could be chronicled at all), though few match the case of John Carter of Lambourn, Berks., who was hanged for arson. At his wish his tombstone records the fact 'as a warning to his companions and others who may hereafter read this memorial'. Undeniably this and many other naive inscriptions now give great pleasure, but we live in a sophisticated age, and an incumbent will naturally want to prevent absurdities. This granted, it remains true that the desire to commemorate remarkable events in this way is a human one, which can add greatly to the interest and value of epitaphs. So, if modern mourners, like their ancestors, want to chronicle outstanding incidents on a memorial ('She was born on the great Ocean in a Storm!' says a monument at Henbury, near Bristol) they should not necessarily be discouraged.

THE GOLDEN RULE

The golden rule is the usual one. The priest should always ask himself whether he would care to be commemorated, or to commemorate others, in a given form of words: he should also ask himself if he would *seriously* object.

13

Disposal After Cremation

Christian teaching has always stressed the dignity of the human body as the temple of the Spirit, hence the manner of its disposal and marking of the spot have been important considerations. The excavation of medieval churchyards has revealed with what care the graves were methodically dug in a deliberate order. Their arrangement is such that there must have been some temporary marker, at the least. This custom of marking the actual site of the burial responds to a deeply-felt wish of the bereaved to know precisely where their beloved is buried.

In recent years the Church has garnered the fruits of her teaching that the churchyard should be the final resting place of the remains of her departed members. As Bishop Healy said: 'The visible church building is incomplete in its witness to this world without this outreach to the dead'. Just as a stone in the churchyard marks the burial of a body so mourners have desired to mark, in the same way, the place where ashes are buried. This satisfies the instinctive desire to *honour* the precise spot; the disposal of remains in the grounds of a crematorium does not provide the same satisfaction, albeit the place is recorded for the future on a map. Sadly, the Church can be said to have become victim of its own success. Many churchyards are experiencing the problem of the proliferation of numerous small tablets laid on the ground adjacent to its pathways and walls. This can create a sizeable paved area quite alien to the nature of a traditional churchyard.

In 1976 we indicated the need for further experiment but, despite many attempts no generally applicable solution has been found. Since 1985 the National Association of Monumental Masons has organised a competition called the Phoenix Award but the commemoration of the interment of cremated remains continues to be an urgent, serious and difficult problem.

There is no doubt that the most practical way for the upkeep of the churchyard is to inter ashes in a marked-out area without any memorial over the spot and for the names to be recorded in a memorial book or on a commemorative roll such as the one we illustrate. In view of people's strong if often unexpressed desire for a locality, however, this is sometimes pastorally difficult to implement. If tablets on the turf have not proved successful, one alternative seems to be a more formal arrangement of tablets in paths or alongside them (as at Penn in Buckinghamshire), or in specially prepared areas expertly laid out by a landscape architect or someone experienced in the various aspects of garden design. Another possibility is to inter ashes within a church building in some kind of columbarium which is in concept, as its name suggests, somewhat akin to a dovecote in providing neatly-arranged separate compartments for ashes in an overall architectural and properly designed context. As an entirely new approach, commemorative tablets, however or wherever located, might be leased, and removed after – say – 25 years or whatever period was agreed.

By referring to the cremated remains as 'ashes', however, as if they were unrelated to the person whose mortal remains they are, we have perhaps unwittingly been party to a process of devaluing the human personality whom we wish to remember and in some way commemorate. Cremated remains are not, in fact, ashes at all, but purified, calcined bone. All that is subject to corruption has been effectively consumed by the 'cleansing power of the flame'.

The failure to deal adequately with the disposal of these remains may in part derive from an unexpressed hope that in due time some form of total combustion would be invented whereby there would, in fact, be no visible or tangible remains at all. Another factor is that, following cremation, all that remains is containable in a small box or urn. It is, therefore, difficult to relate this in scale to a dignified memorial: a normal-sized headstone is generally

KYPIE
REMEMBER
IN PRAYER
Ⱥ BEFORE GOD ⲱ
THOSE WHOSE ASHES
ARE INTERRED IN
THIS CHURCHYARD
ⲈⲖⲈⲎⲤⲞⲚ

Plates 20 and 21.   *Beckley, Oxfordshire: a thoughtful approach to the recording and commemoration of names of those whose cremated remains lie here.*

REMEMBER BEFORE GOD IN PRAYER
the souls of those whose ashes are interred in this churchyard

Harry Newell	1978
Elsie Newell	1980
Hector Wheeler	1982
Kay Alden	1984
Helen Staveley	1985

Be mindful, O Lord, of thy servants and hand maidens who have gone before us with the sign of faith, and do now rest in the sleep of peace.

To them, O Lord, and to all that rest in Christ, grant we beseech thee, a place of refreshment, light and peace, through Christ our Lord. Amen.

ΚΥΡΙΕ ΕΛΕΗΣΟΝ·ΧΡΙΣΤΕ ΕΛΕΗΣΟΝ·ΚΥΡΙΕ ΕΛΕΗΣΟΝ·ΧΡΙΣΤΕ ΕΛΕΗΣΟΝ·ΚΥΡΙΕ ΕΛΕΗΣΟΝ·ΧΡΙΣΤΕ ΕΛΕΗΣΟΝ·ΚΥΡΙΕ ΕΛΕΗΣΟΝ

considered far too large, a miniature one more reminiscent of a pet's cemetery. A larger headstone, or a tablet like the one we illustrate, for the recording of a number of burials may prove satisfactory.

It should probably be the normal practice for the cremated remains of parishioners to be buried in the churchyard ground, in a part of the churchyard deliberately set aside for that purpose, yet not too rigidly defined by dwarf walls, beech hedges, or flower beds. Burials should be in accordance with an orderly plan approved by the PCC from which departures, it should be made clear, are not permitted. A separate register should be kept of these interments. It must be noted that the Local Authorities' Cemeteries Order 1974 requires that there should be no disturbance of cremated remains. The greatest care must therefore be taken over interment as, like coffins, once buried they can only be removed by authority of a faculty.

As to the manner of disposal, it cannot be too strongly urged as a matter of good practice that containers, of whatever kind, should be dispensed with at the actual moment of interment. In many churchyards (and, for instance, the cloister garths or other traditional places of interment associated with cathedrals) this is already a condition firmly laid down. A 'long-life' casket is of no benefit to anyone, except the supplier; and a 'short-life' casket (e.g. of cardboard) or a plastic container will only ensure that the remains tend to adhere together instead of being dispersed into the earth. Direct committal into the earth is, from the point of view of both symbolism and sound practical sense, the course to be preferred. The use of polythene is to be avoided as it is indestructible except by fire.

INTERMENT AREA

It is important to consider each aspect of this matter stage by stage, and the first step must be the setting apart of a specific area of the churchyard for the interment of cremated remains; in conjunction with this step it is necessary to decide upon a means whereby those interred in the area may be commemorated. A faculty will be needed – probably the same faculty can cover other aspects, such as the type of memorial and a display case for a Book of Remembrance in a church – and the advice of the Diocesan Advisory Committee should be sought *before* finally deciding upon what terms to apply for a faculty. The director of the local crematorium may well be able to provide very useful advice. A delegation from or a representative of the Diocesan Advisory Committee with particular knowledge or experience will also usually be willing to visit, and it is an advantage to have the stimulus of an informed outside point of view when deciding upon a matter which is likely to have a considerable effect on the total impact of the church and churchyard, and may involve the disturbance of existing graves or gravestones. All these matters, taken together, will affect the issues which concern a parish priest and parochial church council in the care of their church and churchyard, pastoral, aesthetic and environmental, so it is important to find the best possible solution.

In settling upon the area of the churchyard to be set apart and deciding the manner of demarcation, consideration must be given to the overall impact that this will have. Furthermore, interments near the walls of a church both affect the foundations and cause problems if repairs have to be carried out. It may be well to call in a consultant with special skill in landscape design. Many apparently vacant areas in churchyards conceal both interments and buried headstones. Some have suggested the creation of a sort of grove, with trees in a semi-circle or some other appropriate or symbolic shape and a handsome piece of sculpture, such as may be helpful to prayer or meditation, in the centre. There is also a symbolic association to certain trees or shrubs, which might be planted nearby. Whatever is decided upon, care should be taken to prevent an insensitive change to the general scale of the churchyard and the existing trees and other features that are in it. As far as possible, the demarcation should generally be unobtrusive enough to enable this part of the churchyard to merge more or less imperceptibly into the remainder. As regards its surface treatment, perhaps it is ideal if the grass is just kept reasonably smooth and short but not necessarily to the extent that it will acquire the character of a garden lawn. Interments are then made, as in the grounds of many crematoria, under the turf.

While setting aside of a special area for the interment of cremated remains invariably requires the authority of a faculty, the occasional isolated burial of cremated remains in a part of the churchyard normally used for the burial of bodies may in practice usually be done simply at the incumbent's discretion. Again, it is sometimes desired to bury cremated remains in a grave already occupied by a body, for instance, when the children of a deceased couple wish to bury the cremated remains of one parent in the grave in which the other parent's body lies. There is no objection to this, if it is done at the relatives' request and the incumbent consents, but the cremated remains should be sprinkled in the hole excavated for the purpose and not buried in a casket.

WALL MEMORIALS

Reference has already been made to the very strong instinct on the part of the bereaved to mark the actual place of the interment: and the fact that ideally, from the point of view of those responsible for the upkeep of the churchyard, it is best to have no memorial at all. However, even where there is a rule forbidding this it is frequently the case that the place is marked for a while by a wreath, then later by a posy, and still later, perhaps, with bulbs planted in the turf. Vases, whether temporary or permanent, should be strongly discouraged. A PCC needs to discuss all the possibilities and problems with the Diocesan Advisory Committee and then come to a policy decision which they will afterwards adhere to without wavering.

The 1976 edition of *Churchyards Handbook* made a number of recommendations about tablets. Experience has, however, shown that the size recommended allows inadequate space for the designer's skills, so that there is merely a boring repetition of names and dates. The wedge-shaped stone is also unsatisfactory. Secondly, it has proved almost impossible to keep these stones level, because of problems consequent upon the tilting and sinking of stones. Where rigid adherence to rules of material and style have been applied, there has been a repetitious orderliness; where there has been laxity there is an unsatisfactory untidiness. It seems, therefore, that if one is to allow stones at all, there must be earlier planning and tighter control. For example, it may be possible to prepare a pathway for a number of future interments beneath the surface, or to build alongside a path a low stone kerb for inscriptions. Alternatively, there may be a specially paved path, such as one around a garden seat or in the kind of grove suggested above, with a sculpture as a central ornament. From what has been written above it will be clear that the introduction of tablets creates problems. It may even vitiate in part the purpose of cremation, which is to reduce the area of land taken up by the dead; it may create more maintenance problems. As to the placing of plaques on church walls, little doubt that this is not generally successful and should not be done unless very tightly controlled and unless the artistic standard is high. A large stone containing a number of names might perhaps be better, located on a churchyard wall or close to wherever the cremated remains are interred.

It is worth reiterating the suggestion made above that plaques (either individual or for a group of burials) should be authorised for a fixed period of years only, to introduce an element of recycling after the initial (and very proper) emotional need for commemoration had passed. After this period they would be removed, unless permission were renewed. At Penn, in Buckinghamshire, tablets are turned over after 25 years and new inscriptions cut on the turned side revealed. Note that wherever re-use is contemplated, care must be taken not to disturb the ashes already interred.

BOOKS OF REMEMBRANCE

In many parishes, a Book of Remembrance will be the method chosen. Here it is advisable to consult with both the parish's architect and the Diocesan Advisory Committee, for the book and the stand (probably with a glass top) on which it rests will contribute towards the total impact of the interior of the church itself. It is unlikely that a stock product will provide the most sensitive and appropriate answer – a stand made especially for the setting in which it will be placed (and made, preferably, by a craftsman of some distinction) is a real opportunity for enhancing and enriching the church at a point which will be of comfort to the bereaved and of significance for the whole worshipping congregation. The best, incidentally, is not necessarily the most expensive.

In the Book of Remembrance can be inscribed the names of all those whose ashes have been interred in the churchyard, the cost of the calligrapher's work being added to the fee charged for the interment. The names may be inscribed chronologically or there may be a page to commemorate each day of the year, with the book opened each day at the appropriate page. For the Book to be effective, it should become an integral part of the liturgical furniture. Here flowers can be brought after a cremation; a vase may be provided where people can put flowers on the anniversary of a funeral or a candle may be burned nearby at the time of the Eucharist.

METHOD OF INTERMENT

Sufficient has already been said to make it plain that the use of caskets is not recommended. But what of the actual process of interment? It cannot be too strongly emphasised at this point that *burial* has always been the Christian tradition of decently interring the remains of the departed. 'Scattering' can be unseemly and distressing to the bereaved and this method should normally be avoided. One suggestion is that (having devised an orderly plan for the placing of burial plots in the specially set aside area of the churchyard) a hole should be dug by means of a 6in (150mm) earth auger or post-hole boring tool between 18in (450mm) and 2ft (600mm) deep. The cremated remains will, of course, arrive in some kind of container from the crematorium and the remains should be gently poured into the hole and then *immediately* (to avoid any possible distress to the bereaved) a thin layer of earth sprinkled over the top. If there is a wish to have several interments in the same hole then a stout oak board should be placed over the layer of earth, and the remainder of the hole can be filled in on top of the board as soon as the service of committal has been concluded and the grave plot may then be turfed over. The point of the stout wooden board is that it avoids the possibility of either the cremated remains or the thin layer of soil being disturbed; and it also means that, when the next interment takes place, the topsoil can be removed down to the board, the board lifted up, and the whole process repeated. No ashes should be interred less than 4 inches (100mm) below the surface of the soil. Clearly circumstances will vary from place to place, but this method is strongly recommended as being both seemly and economical in its use of space.

LEGAL QUESTIONS

There can be no objection to the disposal of cremated remains in what is technically a closed churchyard (i.e. closed by Order in Council); occasions may only arise rarely, but if in doubt a faculty should be sought and is likely to be granted, unless the churchyard is being cared for by the local authority and the local authority objects for any reason. Again, this seems unlikely.

If a church itself is consecrated then the curtilage i.e. the area around the building, is also subject to the Faculty Jurisdiction. Sometimes, particularly in urban situations. the ground outside is not consecrated and the church is said to be within 'an *unconsecrated curtilage'*. A bishop may be willing to consecrate the curtilage, if a sufficient need can be shown; but both the Pastoral Measure 1983 and the secular legislation contain provisions enabling churchyards or curtilages, whether consecrated or not, to be devoted to secular purposes in certain circumstances, so there is probably little point in doing this. In any case each situation must be judged entirely on its own merits, and in the first instance it would be wise to seek the advice of the diocesan Registrar.

Disposal of cremated remains in consecrated buildings always, of course, requires a faculty. In the previous edition of the Handbook some hesitation was expressed about the interment of ashes within the church building. However, while we would continue to oppose disposal within the actual walls of a church we are increasingly sympathetic towards interment beneath the floor, provided certain safeguards are met. First the architect must be consulted, and heating or lighting ducts must be left undisturbed; secondly, since any disturbance of the floor may occasion damage to the archaeological evidence, an archaeologist recognised by the diocese (who will usually be the archaeologist member of the Diocesan Advisory Committee) must scrutinise the proposals and satisfy himself that no damage will be done.

The provision of a *columbarium*, especially if there is a crypt, is a possibility which might in certain circumstances be explored. Again early consultation with the church's architect and with the Diocesan Advisory Committee is essential; and a parish must be wary of any proposal which might add to future maintenance responsibilities.

14

The Management of the Natural History of Churchyards Including Guidelines for the Protection of Flora and Fauna

In the past decade there has been a gathering revolution in popular attitudes towards nature conservation, and the churchyard has suddenly come into focus as one of our most important national assets in terms of the habitat it provides for a wide range of grasses, mosses, lichens, ferns, fungi, wild flowers, uncommon introduced flowers, trees (both native and introduced), insects, reptiles, birds and mammals. The country churchyard is in many parishes virtually the sole surviving remnant of ancient herb-rich grassland, enclosed when the church was built or even earlier, and even the town churchyard, crowded with monuments, provides a limited haven for succour for wild life.

The very factors which govern the nature of a churchyard, that is, its setting for what is usually the oldest and most significant building in a community and its function as a safe resting place for the bodies of the dead, are the same which provide the necessary continuity and natural respect to allow a wide range of interdependent flora and fauna to develop and survive.

At every educational level, from the primary school to the most advanced university research institute, the resources of the churchyard have begun to be studied seriously, and form the basis of a growing corpus of published work. At the same time many visitors to churchyards rejoice in the sheer abundance and variety of plant and animal life which can be glimpsed on even a casual visit. Churches and their environs are more visited by tourists than ever before, which brings both more pressure on the delicate balance in a churchyard and – on the other hand – more appreciation and enjoyment. We are a nation of keen gardeners and this means that, while some of the more zealous techniques of gardening are out of place in a churchyard, there is a wide appreciation and knowledge of the plants and trees that grow there: they are closely observed, and a constant source of pleasure.

At the same time the countryside in general is under pressure, and frequently all too vulnerable to the effects of a host of official regulations, to the depredations of encroaching development, and the intensive cultivation of land, using machinery and chemicals. Again, in this context, churchyards represent a resource in terms of ancient or long-established grassland, which is both widely and fairly evenly spread across the landscape, and which is relatively (but not wholly) immune to the changes which have affected the secular landscape.

What is sometimes lacking, and what this chapter seeks to encourage and provide, is a framework for maintenance and management which – while observing the churchyard's primary function as a resting place for the dead – will respect and encourage the diversity of wildlife, in a place where it is entirely appropriate for it to seek sanctuary. A churchyard which is good for wildlife will not be an unbridled wilderness, but can be as neat and attractive as any parishioner could wish.

In this chapter we summarize the nature of the wildlife found in churchyards and itemize the different aspects of maintenance or improvement which need to be taken into account. There is also a list of the specialist organisations which can be turned to for specific advice and help. More detailed information will be found in books listed in the Bibliography.

In brief, there is scarcely a category in the plant or animal life of this country which, unable to grow elsewhere or threatened or fast disappearing, fails to find a home in a churchyard. For example, within the kerb-stones frequently vilified by the adherents of mechanised mowing, there grow not only flowers which have returned to their natural state but also a variety of grasses such as red fescue, tufted hair grass or wavy hair grass. Rare grasses, such as broad-leaved meadow grass, also occur in churchyards here and there. Where conditions are appropriate, certain chalk-loving species are found, such as yellow oat grass or quaking grass. Areas of taller vegetation in parts of the churchyard, allowed to grow alongside graves perhaps, or in isolated corners or at boundaries, provide a habitat for caterpillars; if there is no place for them to grow and pupate there will be no butterflies. Longer grass provides shelter also for the slow-worm, grasshoppers, grass snakes and small mammals.

Churchyards sometimes have a damp area within them, for example in a hollow, and this can be a good habitat for frogs and common toads. In the older parts of churchyards, nothing is more attractive in high summer than the combination of ancient headstones and the surrounding symphony of meadow flowers and grasses. Typical examples are ox-eye daisies, Lady's bed-straw, germander speedwell, bulbous buttercups, common sorrel and mouse-ear hawkweed, amongst a mixture of crested dog's tail grass, meadow grass, cock's foot, foxtail and *Holcus* species, with primrose and lesser celandine in shadier areas. In short, the grassland itself, quite apart from the wild and introduced flowers which give immediate recognition and pleasure, can be surprisingly varied when undisturbed. It should, of course, be the objective of management and maintenance policies to ensure that this remains so. (Constant grazing by sheep or goats is not, without rotation, the real answer; for this would rapidly produce a grassland as dull and poor in species as sheepwalks tend to become.) A very rare aromatic grass, *Hierochloe odorata,* has been found in Scottish churchyards – an appropriate habitat since its folk-name translation is 'holy grass', understandably on account of its odour and location.

Mosses are frequently encountered in churchyards. They are happy growing on, for example, the decaying stumps of felled trees and in damp and shady corners. The only site for the rare moss *Racomitrium aciculare* so far recorded in Surrey is a grave slab in one of its churchyards.

The astonishing variety of *lichens* in churchyards adds greatly to the beauty and interest on the walls of the church and the enclosing walls of the churchyard, as well as the headstones and chest-tombs. Because lowland Britain contains so few natural outcrops of rock, the churchyard is an exceptionally important habitat for those fascinating plants which grow only on stone. Many lichen species have a strong preference for a particular aspect (north, south, east or west), for sunny or shady conditions, or for different building materials – e.g. sandstone, limestone, tiles, bricks, mortar, marble or flint. Old limestone headstones are the most important sites for lichens and the biggest threats to their survival are removal of headstones or their rotation on re-siting so that they face in a different direction. Any use of herbicides in the churchyard is likely also to damage or destroy lichens, which are notoriously sensitive to atmospheric pollu-tants. Moreover, unless disturbed by moving or cleaning, a dated headstone can give a very reasonable idea of the date of a lichen colony, which tends to form fairly quickly when the conditions are favourable, and can be very long-lasting.

Also important in this context are *stonework ferns and flowers*. Three ferns, black spleenwort, wall-rue and maidenhair spleen-wort, and one flowering stonewort plant, pellitory-of-the-wall, have become rare in some parts of the country: in Norfolk, for example, ninety per cent of the surviving population is in churchyards. These are all small and delicate plants with short roots, and there can be no good reason for removing them during repointing or other conservation work to the church or church-yard wall. They are not to be likened to ivy or to tree seedlings in this respect, and deserve to be appreciated and retained.

Wild flowers: the best-known flowers of meadow, wayside and woodland are usually well respected by those who mow the churchyard. Cowslips, primroses, orchids, bluebells and daffo-dils are readily recognisable, and can be avoided. But the wild flower content of the churchyard is likely to be far richer than that, and a first step towards a policy of recognition and conservation is identification. With the ploughing-up or spraying of old meadowland, many meadow flowers have become very dependent on churchyards for survival. Nature Conservancy Council figures show that about ninety-eight per cent of herb-rich meadowland has been lost over the last thirty years. In lowland counties, some meadow flowers have as much as fifty per cent of their surviving populations in churchyards. Conserva-tion measures, as outlined below, are vital to conserve churchyard-dependent species. The work of the county Wildlife Trusts is invaluable in this context, as they are more than willing to carry out botanical surveys and to advise on appropriate methods of management which will respect whatever has been identified.

When a mower is steered round a tree or a sapling, for example, other plants, which may include red campion, white bryony, stitchwort or white comfrey, can take advantage of the shelter provided. In the lawn-like conditions of the more gardenesque parts of the churchyard the slender speedwell will often grow; and, in the protected lee of headstones or under walls protected from the mower, the keeled cornsalad is not infrequent, though distinctly rare elsewhere.

Trees form an indispensable part of the character of a churchyard, for their scale, shade, symbolical associations, practical uses, and their beauty. The yew is the tree species most closely associated specifically with churchyards, and the oldest amongst them may well be the oldest living things in Britain, numbered in thousands rather than hundreds of years. Elms, oaks, beeches and limes were frequently introduced into church-yards from the local woodlands; horse-chestnuts, though neither native nor a woodland tree and comparatively dangerous, were also often introduced. It seems clear from the character of the trees in churchyards which lie within or on the edge of landscape parks, that in the eighteenth and nineteenth centuries the same care was taken, as one would expect, about the planting in the churchyard as in the park, and similarly, just as exotic trees like cedars, Wellingtonia, and monkey puzzles were introduced into parks and large gardens, they were introduced into churchyards. Many notable churchyard trees were planted to celebrate local and national festivals and jubilees; and it is a practice well worth continuing.

Churchyards were consistently enclosed and it is clear that many *hedges* round churchyards are very ancient. Well-established hedges usually contain a wide variety of species. The hedges and the mature trees of a churchyard provide necessary shelter for birds, mammals and insects, especially in those counties and regions where woods and hedges are relatively scarce. In addition, there is evidence to suggest that churches and churchyards in prominent positions provide navigational land-marks and stopping places for some species of migratory birds.

Insects feed on the plant life; in turn, other creatures (for example, birds, bats, amphibia, reptiles and mammals) feed on them. Numerous species of bugs, beetles, flies, caterpillars, butterflies, moths, wasps, bees and crickets flourish in church-yards, not forgetting the universally-loved ladybird. Grassland butterflies (the 'browns', 'common' blue, small copper, etc) are among the insects which have suffered most severely in recent decades, through the use of chemicals in agricultural practice, the ploughing-up, drainage or fertilization of ancient herb-rich grasslands, and the gradual elimination of nettles and other wild shelter and food plants. Many species are nearing total extinction. Again, it is the *interdependence* of all these creatures in the closely-growing churchyard habitat which requires to be stressed.

Bats are a special case, since they are so often encountered in churches and churchyards (though not so often in belfries, which are in general too dusty and too noisy for their comfort). Originally they were animals of cave and woodland, but with the clearance of woodland over the centuries, they came increasingly to live in buildings. Their colonies are usually fairly small: the hostility to them on the part of church cleaners is largely on account of the smell, and the staining and damage which their droppings and urine can cause to textiles, brass and wood furnishings. However, because of the dramatic decline in their numbers and their dependence on buildings for roosting, all bats are now comprehensively protected by the Wildlife and Country-side Act 1981. Any activity that may intentionally kill or injure bats or deny them access to their roosts is illegal. The Nature Conservancy Council must be consulted before any action is taken, in church or churchyard, which may possibly affect bats; it is only too pleased to provide free advice on any matter concerning them. In addition, there are now many flourishing and knowledgeable 'Bat Groups' in different parts of the country, and their volunteer members will usually be willing to investigate any problems and suggest realistic solutions which will not harm the bats. Church porches, as it were poised between the church itself and the churchyard, are places where bats frequently roost;

some species roost in large trees, in the churchyard or elsewhere. The rich insect life of the churchyard is attractive to bats also for their food.

Reptiles have already been mentioned. Slow-worms, declining elsewhere, are able to find sanctuary in churchyards.

Birds of every kind – migrants, common resident species, even birds of specialised habitats like herons, sea-birds and waders – have all been observed in churchyards. The birds which visit or live there appreciate the combination of safe places to roost and a rich variety of food. For the visitor to churchyards or the mourner, the absence of birdsong would be an intolerable deprivation and impoverishment. Among the species frequently recorded in churchyards are tawny and little owls, woodpigeons, tits, swallows, house martins, hedge-sparrows, robins, blackbirds, thrushes, the spotted flycatcher and the woodpeckers. Jackdaws, swifts and kestrels are very typical 'tower birds'. Rookeries are not uncommon and their sepulchral cawing sound seems peculiarly appropriate. The spotted fly-catcher is especially dependent and, with the wren, likes to nest in ivy-covered walls. The barn owl, most lovable of birds, is sometimes referred to as the 'church owl' and fortunate indeed is the church or churchyard where this (now rare) bird resides. Spires, towers and old trees supply the barn owl with suitable hollow places in which to roost and breed its young; quite undisturbed rural churchyards may supply the necessary food and tranquility. Bird-boxes have been successfully introduced into some churchyards, and this is well worth considering as the numbers of all but the most common species of birds have declined alarmingly in recent years.

Mammals, from red deer to foxes and badgers, visit churchyards, and red squirrels occasionally are found living in suitable trees.

How is a conscientious incumbent, churchwarden or parochial church council to deal sensitively and responsibly with the wildlife of the churchyard? Ideally, what is needed is for people in every community combining a sense of what is appropriate for a churchyard with a strong and well-informed appreciation of natural history. The objective should be to create and manage a churchyard environment which is attractive both to all who enter the churchyard and to wildlife. Such an ideal *is* attainable, and is frequently to be found, but understanding and hard work is necessary to formulate a proper policy of maintenance and management.

What follows is a suggested way of approaching the care and maintenance of the principal constituent parts of a churchyard. To avoid the accusation that parts of the churchyard are being 'neglected' it may be desirable to put up a notice stating that part of the churchyard is being managed in such a way as to provide a habitat for scarce plants and other wildlife.

GRASSES AND GRASS CUTTING

In a majority of churchyards it is reasonable to consider grassed areas as falling within these broad categories:

(i) *Paths, and other areas much used by the congregation and by visitors to the churchyard*

These can be mown as frequently as one might mow a lawn, so that there is neatness and good access on the principal routes to the church and the more recent graves. But it should be remembered, nevertheless, that even the neatest parts of a churchyard should not be fertilized and manicured like a garden lawn. The mowing machine chosen should be adaptable (without rollers and with easily adjustable height of mow). If the grass is to be grown long and cut, say, in July, churchyards are going to need at least two sorts of mower, namely both rotary and cylinder, for regular cutting (but probably rotary) and then an Allensey, the type of machine with the hayfield-type 'scissors' cutters for the 'outfield'. However, for the 'outfield' a scythe or swop-hook is preferable. If strimmers must be used, it should be very sparingly, because they cause damage to headstones and to small wild animals, as well as plants. It is best to mow these areas to a length of 38–50 mm, and not shorter; in this way the grass will still be neat, and green throughout the year. A fair variety of grasses can be encouraged, even in a mown lawn; and clover for those places where grass refuses to grow. Daisies, the mouse-ear hawkweed, *Pilosella officinarum,* with its tiny lemon-coloured flowers, and the sky-blue speedwell are among the species happy in closely-mown lawn grasses and on the raised mounds of graves.

(ii) *Areas between older and infrequently visited gravestones*

These areas are best treated as meadow habitat, where the riches of flowering grasses and wild flowers should be allowed to develop and flourish at their best.

The preferred treatment should be to mow less frequently, not more than once a month, and more lightly (to a height of 80 mm). If possible, leave the grass here uncut from the end of April to late June or mid-July, so that the majority of flowers may blossom and perhaps seed.

(iii) *Areas rarely visited and distant from the church*

These should only be mown twice: once in early July, when the hay-making is in progress, and once in September or early October. The bigger plants will flourish here, such as foxgloves, nettles, rosebay willow herb and sorrel (which is a food plant) for the small copper butterfly; small mammals will be left relatively undisturbed. In upland or exposed areas, a single cutting, in August or September, may be quite enough.

(iv) *Crucial principles*

In all this there must be a sense of balance, together with a developing sense of responsibility towards the wildlife community. *Not to cut the grass,* as far as possible, *in May and June* is important, because many of the most churchyard-dependent species (meadow saxifrage, cowslip, pignut) flower then. *At the end of the season* (generally early October) it is good policy *to cut the grass quite short* (50 mm or so). This will give the small delicate species a head start the following spring, without their having to compete with tussocky long grass. Another important point is that *all areas rich in flowers* (or where they are to be encouraged) *should be raked after cutting.* Unless this is done, the decaying grass cuttings will cause a build-up of nutrients which will encourage

Plate 18. *Little Barrington, Gloucestershire: the lichens and algae add an interest of their own to the late medieval tomb-chest.*

vigorous growth of grass and choke all but the most persistent meadow flowers. The aim in planning a cutting timetable should be *to prevent the build-up of coarse tussocky grasses* and keep the grass even-textured. When cutting frequency is eased off, an area may become dominated by unwanted species of vigorous growth (cow parsley, hogweed, stinging nettle); these species are best deterred by cutting (with blades high enough to miss developing flowers and leaves of more desirable species) just as they are beginning to show vigorous upwards growth (for cow parsley this will be around the third week in April, and for hogweed in July).

Finally, and with suitable caveats in mind, there will also be small wild areas, in impenetrable corners or by rubbish heaps, which can be left to themselves to be wholly wild.

It needs emphasizing, though, that a completely unmanaged situation is not in general good for a balanced community of wildlife, and that the rational discriminating approach suggested above should provide conditions variable and satisfactory enough for the comfort and survival both of human beings and of most forms of plant and animal life.

PLANTING FLOWERS AND ESPECIALLY WILD FLOWERS

It is possible that your churchyard has latent within it already a rich and varied collection of species of wild flowers, which will reappear when a mowing regime such as that suggested above has been instituted. But countless churchyards have been improved by the judicious introduction and establishment of plants, and a wonderful enrichment of the churchyard can be achieved by introducing (for example) bluebells, crocus, daffodils, narcissi, winter aconites and snowdrops on graves and allowing them to naturalize. The churchyard of Ashbourne, in Derbyshire, is an outstanding example. If some of the traditional species of wild meadowland and churchyard flowers – such as cowslip, ox-eye daisy or harebell – are absent, then plants can be raised from wild seed in seed-beds or boxes and then planted out. Parishioners are often willing to raise plants for the churchyard from wild species they find in their own garden or farmland and this should be encouraged, especially as these are likely to be of the local genetic stock. If the churchyard has unusual or rare garden plants or trees, it may be worth contacting the county branch of the National Council for the Conservation of Plants and Gardens, c/o R.H.S. Garden, Woking, Surrey GU23 6QB. Advice on appropriate native species can be obtained from the local county Nature Conservation and Wildlife Trust.

HEDGES

Thick hedges provide shelter for birds and many other creatures, including hibernating butterflies and small mammals, and so should be retained as a valuable provider of habitat.

Hedge-laying skills are now comparatively rare, and so (in most cases) machinery will often be needed. It deserves to be widely known that the British Trust for Conservation Volunteers run training courses in hedge-laying, and an excellent handbook is also available. It is sometimes difficult, and probably undesirable, to get hedge-cutting machinery into a churchyard and so it is recommended that even if a mechanical cutter has to used for the top and outside of a hedge, the inside should be cut by hand by a working party of parishioners. A good deal of evidence has reached us on the subject of churchyard working parties: these can be highly enjoyable, and involve more people in a sense of responsibility for the churchyard.

Trimming once a year is quite sufficient. It should be done in March, if the hedge provides fruits for wintering birds, in August-September for non-fruit-bearing hedges, so that there will be a good spread of green foliage through the winter, to provide shelter for over-wintering insects (e.g. the brimstone butterfly). Pale oak bush cricket etc. enter the hedge in October so will not be destroyed during hedging. Never cut in spring when birds may be nesting. Handclipping is to be preferred to machinery, again deploying groups of volunteers if possible. It is easier to get a larger group of people together for a big effort on two or three days a year than to get a smaller group of people together once a fortnight, and it is much more fun!

It is recommended that hedges should be trimmed to an A-shape, thick at the base, thereby preserving their value as a habitat, and narrow at the top, cut at a height of 6-8 feet; at this height, hedges can support the nests of some ten bird species. Care should be taken not to destroy bindweed, honeysuckle and bryony which may be growing in the hedges. It is desirable to preserve a few feet of uncut grass, or infrequently cut grass, next to the hedge, as cover for small mammals such as voles, as well as amphibia and reptiles. If hedges require repair or replanting, it may be worth checking with the district and county councils to see if there are grants available to assist with the planting of trees and hedges. Indigenous trees should be planted when opportunities occur, and pressure to plant exotic conifers or foreign flowering species should be firmly resisted. Hazel, holly, hawthorn, viburnum, bird cherry, crab apple and beech are among the native species which do well in a hedge. It is essential not only to plant them well but to provide adequate after-care (e.g. keep weeds away from the roots, keep roots moist when there is no rain, plant with bond or seaweed meal, and water occasionally with a liquid seaweed fertilizer, which promotes good strong root growth).

TREES AND SHRUBS (see also separate chapter on 'Trees')

Trees and shrubs, like hedges, provide shelter and food for birds, insects and bats.

It is recommended that trees should be left to themselves unless they are plainly becoming a nuisance or unsafe: they should be discouraged from growing too close to the church itself or the churchyard wall, in case structural or foundation damage is caused and gutters become choked in autumn. If the condition of a tree causes concern then the tree officer of the local authority should be consulted for free advice. Many churchyards contain trees which are the subject of a Tree Preservation Order (TPO), which is a signal that the tree should in most circumstances be preserved in just the same way as a listed building or structure of special architectural or historic interest, such as a tombstone, lych-gate or churchyard walls. If, for some reason, a tree which is the subject of a TPO is proposed for felling, then this must be authorized in writing by the local planning authority before any work can proceed. Permission may, of course, be refused.

In planting trees or shrubs, as with hedges, native species are to be preferred, see the separate chapter on trees for specific suggestions.

District and county councils should be approached about the possibility of grants to assist in tree-planting. Valuable advice may also be forthcoming from the Forestry Commission. If you are near a regional headquarters of the National Trust or the county Wildlife Trust then, equally, advice and help may be available there – opportunities to build bridges between the church authorities and the various independent and outstandingly successful conservation trusts should never be neglected.

GRAVE PLANTING AND GENERAL GARDENING IN THE CHURCHYARD

Planting on graves is an ancient tradition and there has been something of a revival of this attractive custom. In planting bulbs and other flowers on a grave it is important that people should decide for themselves but, since suggestions are often asked for, semi-wild flowers, plants which will 'naturalize' themselves, and herbs, are all seemly and appropriate. Excellent examples are snowdrops, bluebells, daffodils, primroses, cowslips, rosemary, lavender and other sweet-scented herbs. Other possibilities are heartsease pansy, Solomon's seal. Our Lady's mantle, autumn crocuses and, as ground cover, periwinkle, variegated dead nettle, cotoneaster *horizontalis* or ivy – of which there are many varieties.

SOURCES OF ADVICE AND HELP

Reference has already been made to several sources. Surveys by the local recorder of the Botanical Society of the British Isles are also particularly valuable, and recorders may often be able to identify plants which may be rare or need special care. In some counties the Wildlife Trust or Botanical Society recorder will already have some surveys or have produced a management leaflet.

Every churchyard, however small or large, should have a proper *plan* for its maintenance and management, written down, and from time to time debated by the parochial church council, and this should be subject to periodic review and amendment. Generally speaking, though, it should take the long-term rather then the short-term view and always keep in mind the special character of a churchyard. Continuity of management over the years is also important, to allow species to flourish. A good first source of advice, for the basis of such a plan, will be the local Wildlife Trust. A representative should be invited to visit, assess, report and advise on the management policy and plan. The national address, from which the local one may be obtained, is: Royal Society for Nature Conservation, 22 The Green, Nettleham, Lincoln LN2 2NR.

Advice on bats should be sought, in the first place, from the Nature Conservancy Council, Northminster House, Peterborough PE1 1WA. The NCC will be able to advise on other aspects of nature conservation in churchyards.

There are also specialist societies for mosses and liverworts, reptiles and amphibia, fungi, molluscs and insects, and the addresses of their secretaries may be obtained from the British Museum (Natural History), Cromwell Road, London SW7 5BD.

Other useful addresses are:

The Botanical Society of the British Isles,
c/o Department of Botany,
British Museum (Natural History),
Cromwell Road,
London SW7 5BD.

British Lichen Society,
Conservation Officer,
Dr A. A. Dalby,
Department of Botany,
Imperial College,
Prince Consort Road,
London SW7 5BB.

Fauna and Flora Preservation Society,
c/o Zoological Society of London,
Regents Park,
London NW1 4RY.

Royal Society for the Protection of Birds,
The Lodge,
Sandy,
Beds SG19 2DL.

15

Trees

Trees are important features in a churchyard. They create a restful atmosphere, and give shelter from harsh winds and summer sun to birds and churchyard visitors alike. Often it would be difficult to imagine a particular church without its familiar trees. Because of this, we tend to take them for granted, but it is important to realise that they are living organisms which grow, flourish, decay and die and in due course have to be removed. Most of the specimen trees seen in churchyards today were planted by previous generations: it is the duty of each generation not only to safeguard them but to plan and plant for the future. We do not have to wait for well-loved trees to be felled because they have become old and dangerous before planting their successors.

It is a useful exercise to list all the trees in the churchyard and consider each one of them in the light of both the present and the future.

THE PRESENT

Are there enough trees or is your churchyard a prairie? There are probably places where tree-planting could create variety, texture and shelter. Are there too many trees, making parts of the churchyard overcast? Are any of them becoming dangerous, or throwing too much shade, or causing damp, or damaging walls, buildings or memorials? Should any be removed or lopped? Certain trees may have been listed for protection by the local authority by means of a Tree Preservation Order (TPO) and it is essential to be aware which trees are so protected.

THE FUTURE

What will each tree look like in twenty years' time, in fifty, in a hundred? Will it have died, or will it have to be removed? Should new trees be planted now, or in the future, to replace existing trees which may disappear?

Seedling trees or suckers of ash, yew, hawthorn and wild rose usually augment the planted stock of trees in a churchyard. Often these may be encouraged, but where they are in an inconvenient place 'coppicing' is an alternative. This entails cutting the trunk back to the ground every few years – it will grow again to make a bushy many-stemmed small tree, and the cut stems can be put to use.

Trees in churchyards may not be felled without the consent of the Diocesan Parsonages Board. An exception is when an emergency arises: if such a case occurs, the Archdeacon should be consulted (see chapter on Churchyards and the General Law).

Felling of large trees in confined spaces is a difficult and dangerous job which must be carried out by experts.

It is worth getting good advice before contemplating any felling, planting or topping. There is often a woodlands officer attached to local district or county councils. In country districts many private or National Trust estates employ woodmen or foresters who are very knowledgeable. Local authorities' parks departments will also be able to provide expert advice. Forestry consultants exist and there are reputable tree surgeons and nurserymen. The Forestry Commission's officers and foresters may be ready to advise in an unofficial and friendly capacity. Get more than one opinion if you are in doubt.

The planting of new trees and subsequent care of them is not difficult but requires forethought. Scale is an important factor. How will the tree look when it is fully grown? Will it be too close to the church or the churchyard boundary or adjoining houses? Will it harm existing memorials? Perhaps a small tree such as whitebeam or rowan might be suitable where a large one would take up too much room in its maturity. If there is room, there is a lot to be said for planting big, long-lived trees, either individually or in groups or lines, to provide beauty and pleasure for several centuries.

Care should be taken over the planting. A nice deep hole is essential, into which a handful of bonemeal and some compost is placed; the stake goes in first, then the tree; the hole is gently backfilled with good soil, and all is stamped down firmly. The tree is tied to a stake which should reach one-third of the way up the trunk or 2-2½ feet from the ground, and then a rabbit guard must be fixed. It is recommended that the traditional practice (which is also good conservation practice) of planting large trees only round the edge of the churchyard be adhered to; most significant churchyard plants, including the meadow flowers and lichens, need sunny conditions; shrub species are best planted in patches in corners of the churchyard for the same reason. In a small churchyard there are plenty of smaller but still beautiful species to choose from.

Whether evergreen or deciduous trees, conifers or broad-leaved should be chosen is a matter of judgment in individual circumstances. Trees should harmonise with their surroundings and with each other. Deciduous trees have the advantage of looking different at each season of the year and the native species usually look better in the churchyard setting. Evergreens give shade, shelter and colour all the year round. If there is room for both, so much the better. From the point of view of nature conservation, native broad-leaved trees should be the first to be considered. Most broad-leaved trees are deciduous (exceptions being the holly and the holm-oak) and autumn leaf-fall may have to be dealt with by sweeping leaves off paths and out of gutters; but this is a small price to pay for the beauty of autumn colouring. Most conifers are evergreen (an exception is larch).

Individual tree species have different requirements as regards light and shade, soil, moisture or dryness, shelter or exposure and purity of air. There are many books available on the subject – some are listed at the end of this publication. It is not possible to deal in full here with individual species, but one or two notes may be useful.

The traditional churchyard tree is the yew, and many churchyards contain ancient yews. Their value and significance cannot be over-estimated. Many are important historically, and they are often of considerable, even exceptional, antiquity. The churchyard yew at Fortingale in Perthshire is said to be 1,500 years old, and there are countless trees in England and Wales whose age can be reckoned in hundreds of years. If there seems to be a problem, a tree specialist should be consulted. A yew should not be considered dead even if there is no appearance of life; it may regenerate after several years. A hollow trunk should never be used as a dumping place or as an incinerator, nor should it be filled with brick and cement.

In the mass, yews may strike some people as a little gloomy, but it was a tree which traditionally conferred protection from evil. Their dark green foliage contrasts admirably with the building materials of our churches, and the custom of planting churchyard yews should be encouraged and preserved. Remember, however, that on no account should livestock have access to yew trees, which are poisonous, and should not be allowed to overhang adjoining fields. The old form of yew is a spreading tree and it would be nice to see more of these being planted; the more upright or fastigiate form is seen everywhere in drives and avenues. It is important to specify the spreading form, if you intend to plant one: that is, *Taxus baccata* (the Irish yew is *Taxus baccata Fastigiata*).

Of our conifers, apart from the many decorative and garden varieties available, Scots pine is hardy and attractive when well grown. Cedars must have plenty of room and are slow growing, but old trees, especially cedars of Lebanon, can be magnificent and are worth considering. True cypresses are not fully hardy in Britain; Leyland and other false cypresses are not good as true-specimen trees.

Small-leaved lime, beech, rowan, horse-chestnut, field maple and sycamore are good native trees for churchyards. Oak is a traditional English tree, but has no particular decorative virtues in this context. Elms, until some variety immune to Dutch elm disease is developed, are unreliable in their habits and are best avoided (other than small weeping varieties). Ash can be very beautiful and let sunlight through their foliage, but, like sycamore, they encourage seedlings, which may become a problem. Among the smaller trees, silver birch is graceful and attractive, as are whitebeam and rowan. Flowering cherries and almonds should be planted sparingly. The virtues of holly, a tree which has religious associations, should not be overlooked; with dense shiny evergreen leaves and winter berries (on the female tree only), holly is a traditional churchyard tree. Do not plant large, fast-growing species of tree near buildings – especially those built on shrinkable clay. A famous lawsuit resulted in an award of damages in respect of the effects of poplar roots on a next-door neighbour's house. However, in open ground, the balsam poplar is a fast-growing tree, with bright glossy leaves which shed their beautiful resiny fragrance throughout the churchyard.

There are many churchyards which would benefit from the wise planting of smaller trees, and it may be possible to get financial assistance from the Countryside Commission via the county council. If you need to order a minimum number remember that you can include species for hedging such as hawthorn, and that guelder rose, hazel and wayfaring trees make good bushy screens or hedges and can be kept to 6–8ft high by coppicing. In all cases advice should be sought from people knowledgeable about trees to ensure that they are not planted where their roots will undermine the church or churchyard walls, or interfere with gravestones or with grave-digging. Care should also be taken that their leaves do not fill gutters or down-pipes; and the tree or trees chosen should be complementary to the church and its existing surroundings in scale, type, and location. Parishioners often seek ways of commemorating relatives: a tree in the churchyard is a most attractive way of achieving this.

In the early months and years of the life of a tree care must be taken to keep the surrounding area clear of weeds – you can mulch with churchyard grass cuttings. Take care to avoid damage when mowing grass nearby. Planting small trees and indicating their presence with a rabbit guard is usually successful; if larger trees are planted, use a low stake and remove it after a few years.

The commoner trees are not expensive to buy, at any rate not in small sizes, and it is worth noting that small trees are established more easily than bigger ones, whose growth they often overtake in a few years. They need protection from rabbits, hares, sheep and dogs. If you get a grant for your trees, it is likely that it will also partly fund rabbit guards.

It is surprising and disturbing to discover how few people professing to be able to prune or pollard trees really understand how to do it. It might be useful for Diocesan Advisory Committees and rural deans to compile lists of recommended firms or individuals.

The sylvicultural beauty of our churchyards over the next century depends upon the trouble we are prepared to take today. The planting and care of trees is one of the most rewarding activities involved in the care of churchyards, and one of the best contributions a churchyard can make to its wider surroundings and to the community.

16

Recording the Churchyard

It is extremely important to keep a full record of all burials in the churchyard. The Faculty Jurisdiction Commission has recommended that a plan of graves should be required by law, and stressed that much fuller records than a mere plan are also highly desirable. The plan should mark all extant monuments. Unmarked graves that can be identified, perhaps by low mounds, should be recorded as such and be marked on the plan, as should the sites of cremation of any churchyard no longer in use. Where gravestones, or even parts of monuments such as kerbstones, are to be removed or have their positions altered then a record should be made. We hope that applicants for the necessary faculty required for this work will be ordered to provide a survey as a record, comparable to that outlined below. The Council for British Archaeology are to produce a new practical handbook on recording graveyards in 1989.

The churchyard plan should be made at a scale which allows location of a grave to within 30 cm. It should therefore not be smaller than a scale of 1:250, and is much better at 1:100. The church architect may have a suitable base plan of the churchyard, or at least of the church, which will be a base from which to work. It is not easy to produce a detailed, accurate plan, especially if the churchyard is large or slopes steeply. If possible, expert assistance should be sought from the local museum, archaeological unit or technical college. The last may be able to carry out the plan as a student surveying exercise, but it is necessary to ensure that the final result is sufficiently accurate. The plan must show the outline of the church and any other buildings within the churchyard, all paths, trees and flower beds as well as the burials. Clearance of excessive vegetation is often necessary before a full record can be made; old recumbent slabs in particular can be difficult to locate, and broken memorials have often been put in some peripheral, neglected part of even the apparently well-kept churchyard. If the grass is cut short then the labels that identify monuments during the survey are easy to locate, as are the undulations indicating unmarked graves.

If a survey is to be carried out without expert assistance, basic surveying books should be consulted from the local public library. Surveyor's tapes can be used to measure out from fixed points on the church and boundary wall and in this way paths, major monuments and trees can be plotted using offsets over short distances and otherwise by triangulation and 3:4:5 triangles. The tapes may be borrowed from a local school, technical college, museum, estate agents or architects. Gradually more and more detail can be added until all monuments have been accurately surveyed. With large churchyards difficulties will be encountered in areas some distance from known points. Here special care must be taken to double check since cumulative errors are frequent. Where discreet areas have been added to the graveyard, and may even be detached, separate plans may be desirable. In such cases, ensure that north is marked on all plans and it is clear how the various parts fit together. All plans should be labelled with the name of the church and parish, have the scale, the date of the survey and names of the surveyors clearly marked.

The plan should be drawn on durable material, and plastic drafting film is recommended. The final result can be inked in using a drawing pen, and dye-line copies can then be produced and further annotated if necessary. The church architect may be able to supply materials and produce copies. It is desirable, however, to update regularly the original on the drafting film so that new burials are not only recorded on a relatively imperma-nent dye-line.

Each grave should be given a number which relates to the plan and any record forms, even if there is no extant memorial. It is wise to number in a systematic way, moving along rows and gradually around the graveyard. Each grave number should be indicated with a temporary label; white plastic garden tags have proved suitable. After the stones have been recorded and the detailed plan has been made, then the labels can be taken up. If white labels are considered unsightly, lollipop sticks are also effective, but are more difficult to find during the survey. If a grid can be superimposed onto the plan, each monument can be given a grid reference which will allow easy location on the plan, particularly as new memorials are added to the graveyard and to the records. The advantage of using plastic drafting film for the base plan is that it can be placed over graph paper and a grid easily constructed. This should be clearly marked all round the edge of the plan.

Every memorial should be recorded on a standard form. (For a specimen see Appendix V). The advantage of having an A4 form is that it is easy and relatively cheap to photocopy or have printed. The forms can then be stored in a ring-binder in numerical order. The most obvious element is the inscription, and this should be carefully transcribed, set out line by line as on the stone. Upper and lower case should be used as on the inscription but the style of lettering should not be imitated. It is vital to write extremely legibly. Inscriptions on different parts of a memorial (for example the headstone and kerbs) should be put on the same form which should be annotated to make this clear. If the inscription is long, it can be continued on the back of the form. Where parts of the inscription are illegible, this should be indicated by leaving appropriate gaps. Great care must be taken over the reading of numbers, particularly on eighteenth-century memorials. The sides and the back of gravestones may have additional inscriptions, including the name of the monumental mason. Often older stones are now partly buried, and as much of the inscription should be recorded as is possible without undue excavation.

Other information about each monument should also be recorded, including meaurements, orientation (using a compass), style of lettering, shape, decoration and the materials from which it was made. This must be collected in a uniform manner, and for this reason it is desirable that a code sheet is prepared for all recorders, by which letters can be used as abbreviations on the form. On matters such as geology it is advisable to allow someone with some expertise to fill in this section of every form. Make sure that a copy of the code sheet is kept with all the records.

The recording form and associated coding sheet which has been tried and tested in the survey of over twenty graveyards in Pembrokeshire, Dyfed is given in Appendix V. Whilst this may form a basis for other graveyard records, it is important to adapt the coding categories to local circumstances. A thorough examination of the contents of the churchyard will enable any appropriate alterations to the coding to be made. Without doubt the most vital point is accuracy and consistency in recording, at whatever level of detail is considered feasible. The Pembrokeshire recording form was designed to allow quick and accurate recording in the field, followed by subsequent further coding based on information supplied from the inscription so that archaeological and historical analysis could be undertaken. The primary record of the memorial is that recorded by the transcribed inscription, the photograph and by the code information as far down as decorated motifs. The categories below the line are derived from the inscription, and need not be filled in unless for local historical research. For example, that labelled 'People commemorated' is to record the ages and dates of death for demographic analysis. The ways in which these other parts of the form can be filled in, and how the data can be studied manually or using a small microcomputer, is discussed in the forthcoming Council for British Archaeology handbook. There is no need to go into further detail here since the concern is the primary recording, not the analysis, of the churchyard.

All transcriptions and codings should be checked by at least one other person since mistakes are easily made, especially if many forms are being filled in by the same person during one day. In the Pembrokeshire surveys, up to thirty stones could be recorded by one individual in a day, but much depends on the condition of the stone and the length of the inscription.

Each monument should also have a photographic record. This is the most expensive part of any survey, and may be undertaken over a period of time. Whilst colour prints are easy to get commercially processed, they have a relatively short archival life and are not recommended if black and white photographs can be obtained. There should be some amateur photographers who would be prepared to take part in the survey. A 35 mm or larger format camera should be used, since the resolution from smaller negatives is not sufficient for the required detail. Whilst a photographer is available it may be advisable for a good range of photographs to be taken inside the church, and particularly close-ups (with a scale) of any movable objects such as carved stones and furniture. Such photographs are invaluable to the police if any items are subsequently stolen.

The photographs should be taken when oblique light falls on the inscribed face, ideally from the top left. If sunlight never directly strikes the stone then the use of indirect flash is recommended. Even fragmentary and heavily eroded monuments should be photographed as a record. Flash from various angles can highlight different parts of a worn inscription and allow more to be read from the prints than may be possible directly from the stone. Some complex memorials might also require more than one photograph, with views from several sides. It is of course better to err on the side of over-photographing the memorials, but most will need only one picture. Each composition should include a scale (such as a 30 cm ruler suitably painted to be readily visible) and the memorial number which may be written clearly on a small blackboard. Both the scale and board can be propped up next to the stone, clearly visible but not covering any vital part of the monument. The inclusion of the number is essential to prevent confusion over identifying photographs and collating them with the recording forms at a later date. Prints should be made of each memorial, and affixed to the recording forms. Where there is more than one print, the additional pictures can be fixed to the back of the form.

It is highly desirable that more than one set of records is made. Each set should consist of the plan, the record forms with photographic prints and the code sheet. One set can be kept in the church safe, another at the diocesan record office and, ideally, a further set at the local library. The original plan on drafting film should be kept at the church but should only be rolled up, not folded. Every few years new copies of the plan and copies of additional record sheets for new or rediscovered graves should be sent out so that all the sets are kept fully up to date. It is advisable that the photographic negatives should be placed in archivally stable negative holders and deposited at the diocesan record office for safe keeping.

17

Designing Alterations and Improvements

This chapter covers various aspects of design in relation to the alteration and improvement of existing churchyards, including their extensions; and it includes also some suggestions on the design aspects of providing new or additional parochial burial grounds.

GENERAL

It must be at once admitted that it is not an easy matter to give broad advice on design matters which will be equally helpful or applicable in all places and in all circumstances. Just as William Morris's famous dictum 'Stave off decay by daily care' is arguably the best advice ever given on the care of buildings (whether old or new), so Alexander Pope's advice 'Consult the genius of the place in all' (*Epistle to Lord Burlington,* line 57) is surely the most sensible approach to any matter of design which touches on the landscape or townscape qualities of any particular place. This is the first important point to bear in mind. A churchyard or burial ground, whether ancient or new, is not an event in itself: it is, by its purpose and its context, inescapably a part of the community to which it belongs and in design terms it ought not to appear like an alien or uncomfortable intrusion, but like a harmonious and indeed specially beautiful part of the whole.

Because, as we have argued elsewhere, the proper provision for the disposal and remembrance of our dead is a vital part of the experience of grief, any change or alteration should be one for the better in those terms. In other words, although practical considerations may be deserving of attention, they should not be allowed to have absolute priority over questions of good taste, sensitivity, or decorum. To give a specific instance: many churchyards have ancient and mellow paths of cobbles, or of paving stones, and the temptation to replace or cover them with tarmacadam should be firmly resisted. As with all aspects of buildings, tried and tested and traditional materials not only look better but also generally last much longer. What they need is regular maintenance and occasional repair, rather than replacement or obliteration.

A useful proposition to bear in mind is that the enlarging of a churchyard, or its alteration or extension, or the provision of a new one is an aspect of good landscape or (in a special sense) garden design and professional people skilled in those fields should at once be consulted if changes are being considered. The parish architect (i.e. the architect who carries out the Quinquennial Inspection Report and collaborates with the parish in the care of the church fabric) should also be consulted, as he will certainly have helpful advice to give, and if new design work is needed he may well be the most appropriate person to provide it.

ENCLOSING WALLS

It has always been both a canonical requirement and a matter of common sense that churchyards should be properly enclosed, whether by a ditch, hedge, fence, or wall. For late twentieth-century purposes it is likely that a hedge or a wall will be the most effective and also, if well considered, the most attractive option. Advice is given on hedges in the chapter on Flora and Fauna; for walls, it is appropriate to consider the material of which the church itself is built and the nature of the local vernacular or predominant architecture. To be specific, a brick, stone or flint churchyard wall naturally looks well when it is perceived as the setting for a brick, stone or flint church. A deliberate contrast, if thoughtfully considered as to colour and texture, may also work well. There are also the happy accidents of history. For example, at Wingham in Kent, the churchyard wall is largely (as one would expect) of flint; but, in the seventeenth century, an extensive area on the eastern boundary was rebuilt in red brick with the date '1637' picked out in different coloured bricks, and the result is delightful. At Penn, in Buckinghamshire, it was possible to provide an extension to the ancient churchyard by adding on to it the adjacent eighteenth-century vineyard already enclosed in mellow red brick. The contriving of the new entrance-arch added an attractive feature, whether seen from the old churchyard or the new.

It is noticeable how in the nineteenth century church and churchyard, including entrance gates and possibly a lych-gate as well, were conceived of as a group. This is a good principle to follow, particularly if the areas concerned are fairly small. But many larger churchyards, perhaps extended several times over the centuries like that at Carshalton in Surrey, are like a series of large outdoor rooms and this is an equally acceptable way of approaching the question of adding to an existing churchyard or providing a new one if it is done with awareness. The several different areas will, in most cases, tend naturally to have a character varying from one another insofar as they have to respond to the exigencies of the site – e.g. whether it is flat or sloping, or constrained by existing boundaries or buildings or other features. As in the design of a good large garden (which, in a certain sense, a churchyard so much resembles) the provision of enclosing walls will take into consideration the advantages both of congruity and of pleasing surprise and skilfully contrived contrast.

ENTRANCE GATES

It should be regarded as axiomatic that a churchyard should have a proper entrance or, if the site and context demand, two or more entrances, one of which will probably be the principal entrance. Gate-piers (as with the handsome pairs of eighteenth-century stone gate-piers at Malpas in Cheshire) add immeasurably to the dignity and identity of a churchyard. Although the idiom chosen will depend on many factors it is worth noting that, as at Malpas, a classical idiom works well with a gothic church and there are today many architects who can skilfully handle the classical vocabulary; if the chosen idiom is 'contemporary' then it should at least avoid being either aggressive or unfriendly towards the church building itself.

The provision of gates, whether of wood or of metal, provides a marvellous opportunity for commissioning a local craftsman – or indeed, for that matter, one of national repute – to make something special. There have already been excellent examples of this – for example Bryant Fedden's gates and gate-piers at Tewkesbury Abbey in Gloucestershire – and it is much to be encouraged. The cost can be high or low, the concept simple or lavish depending on the circumstances, provided something good, serviceable and attractive is achieved. 'Commodity, firmness, and delight' are still highly appropriate ideals for any new design work, and it should be borne in mind that we live at a time when more people than ever (their eyes attuned by television to the effect of frequent debate on architectural matters in the press) are concerned at the visual quality of our environment. It is not at all fitting that the appearance, design or maintenance of a churchyard or burial ground should lag behind in this respect. The provision of new work, whether by improvement or addition, should be regarded as a real opportunity to do the very best that can be achieved. Moreover families, whether individually or collectively, are often anxious to give something appropriate by way of a memorial – and what can be more appropriate than a handsome pair of entrance gates, or some other specific feature of the churchyard where a loved one lies buried?

LYCH-GATES, SUNDIALS, SCULPTURE

Much the same can be said of lych-gates or other special features. All over the country inscriptions on lych-gates bear testimony to the fact that their erection was an act of generosity by families to commemorate a particular person or indeed by a whole parish, to commemorate a former incumbent, for example, or as a war memorial. A relatively simple lych-gate, of traditional carpentry and roof-covering, need not be outrageously expensive and in certain circumstances it would be a wonderful contemporary addition to the dignity and beauty of a churchyard.

Again, the provision of a sundial – not 'off the peg', but preferably by a good local sculptor – can be an enjoyable addition to a churchyard, perhaps with a suitable text. Its symbolism is peculiarly apt, and a sundial can be an ideal centrepiece for an area set aside for the interment of cremated remains.

In gardens, whether large or small, a piece of sculpture (or a special tree or shrub) can be tellingly deployed as a focus for meditation or as a pivot in the design. The same is true of churchyards. This is beautifully demonstrated also at Penn, where the churchyard extension has a fine centrepiece by the local sculptor, Darsie Rawlins, recalling ancient medieval churchyard crosses but in a twentieth-century idiom. On one side a dove represents the Holy Spirit, and on the other is a Mother and Child image. Such symbolism and such images can be a real inspiration to mourners and other visitors, to enhance the feeling of the churchyard as a very special place, and not (as sometimes seems to be the case) an untidy corner of a field where bodies happen to be buried.

PATHS

Much of the beauty and seemliness of a churchyard depends on its paths.

A clear distinction can be made between paths to the main church doors and those surrounding the church or leading to a side entrance. The main path should be wide enough for a coffin to be carried comfortably – 5 to 6 feet (1.5 to 1.8 m) is a fair width – and side-fencing should be avoided. If the path is too narrow, people are encouraged to walk on the grass. It is often economically impossible to surface side-paths but these can sometimes be left and kept regularly mown.

While old paving should be scrupulously retained, the main approaches must be kept in safe condition for pedestrians. A hard gravel path is traditional in some districts; in others, flat stones or bricks are used, sometimes with a border of another material such as cobblestones or flints. A good deal of paving of this type is very old; it is important that local traditions of path-making or paving should be retained. Ornamental tiled edges are out of place, unless traditional. Weeds in gravel paths can be destroyed by Prefix granules or by watering with a solution of sodium chlorate in the proportion of 4 oz to 1 gallon (110 grams to 4.5 litres) of water. Algae can be removed from stone flags by an application of a very weak solution of 'Domestos'. Care must be taken, as this solution will burn grass. Weeds in brick and stone-paved paths are most easily destroyed with a flame-gun.

When repaving or relaying churchyard paths, a careful watch should be kept for interesting and valuable monumental slabs, turned out of the church and used either as paving or foundations of paths. The mensa of a pre-Reformation altar or the indented slabs of memorial brasses are not uncommon finds.

PCCs should be urged to make a path all round but not too close to the church. It is important to be able to walk round the building in all weathers, as neglect and untidiness, unsightly sheds and rubbish heaps are most usual where they are not readily seen. Moreover, stopped gutters and gullies and signs of decay will be more readily observed if inspection is carried out regularly.

Ashes, clinkers, and smooth tiles should not be used to make paths in churchyards for sound practical reasons, but in brick-country, ordinary walling bricks are satisfactory. Concrete is tolerably satisfactory if roughly mixed.

Paths should not be excessively cambered; examples exist, unfortunately, in beautiful old churchyards of paths relaid on a steep camber with concrete scored with a trowel to imitate crazy-paving.

In urban context, if cost is an over-riding consideration and there is no better material available, tarmac with a flush border of slabs or bricks may sometimes be used, but road metal macadam or gravel, well rolled, is to be preferred, as it dries quickly after rain. Tarmac in a country churchyard *never* looks well, but its blackness can be tempered if gravel is rolled into it as a top dressing. Once more, we should 'consult the genius of the place in all' and avoid anything inharmonious or harsh in colour, contrast or texture.

SHEDS AND RUBBISH PLACES

It is highly desirable, for both aesthetic and sound practical reasons, that the church itself should be kept unencumbered by toolsheds, rubbish heaps and fuel-stores and the like. All these things are necessary, but there is no need for the appearance of the church and churchyard to be spoiled by the erection of various temporary and makeshift structures and ill-placed dumps, as can so readily happen without forethought and vigilance.

In many churches, fuel and tools are accommodated in a seemly and permanent manner under cover, either inside the boiler house, or in a screened-off portion of the vestry; but where they are not, what may be required is a small structure in a corner of the churchyard or against the churchyard wall, away from the church, to serve for tools or storage. There is no need for it to be expensive, though wood is no longer cheap, and it need not be made to look 'Gothic' or 'ecclesiastical'. Canadian red cedar makes a pleasant-looking shed if good design is chosen, and the materials can readily be bought. This wood needs no preservative, and usually harmonizes well with its surroundings. Corrugated iron should be avoided.

It may be found impractical to provide a shed for solid fuel, which after all does not deteriorate with exposure, but in no case should fuel be allowed to stand against the church itself. Rainwater percolating through it is likely to produce a harmful chemical reaction which will cause serious decay in stone or brick, and the heap itself will probably bridge any damp course.

The siting of storage tanks presents a problem to parishes converting to oil-fired heating. These tanks are necessarily large, but it is sometimes possible to find room for them in the former boiler house. If, however, a tank is to be sited actually in or under the church, it should be placed in a proper fire-resisting compartment and above a catchpit, and only after architectural advice has been given and considered. If a tank is to be placed outside the church, in an existing lean-to compartment, care should be taken to ensure that there are no unprotected openings in the church wall at this point, which in case of a fire would permit the rapid spread of heat and fumes. If the tank is to be in the open air, it should be within a suitable catchpit, preferably a few feet away from the church to allow repainting all round. A position should be found which is inconspicuous, and not too far away from the boiler. It can be screened by planting. It is not necessary for the tank to be placed in a prominent position near the road, since the tankers in which the fuel is delivered are equipped with long hoses. If, however, it is more than 80 or 90 feet (24 or 28 m) from the nearest point of access, it will probably be necessary to lay a filling-pipe to a point nearer the road.

The priming coat of paint which is usually applied when the tank is delivered is quite inadequate to prevent rust forming. It should be given two coats of paint before it is fixed in position on blue brick or concrete piers. Bitumastic paint can be obtained in pleasant grey or dull russet shades and black. Black makes the tank appear least conspicuous.

Water tanks should not be allowed to remain against the walls of churches, unless this is the only possible means of supply, as they frequently leak unnoticed and cause walls to become damp. Provision for water supply should preferably be made by a standpipe elsewhere in the churchyard. Sometimes, however, water can only be obtained by collecting it from the roof of a shed or of the church itself. The water is then often stored in a metal tank, although suitably coloured plastic butts are now available, either without an overflow pipe or with one which is inadequate. A good supply can be obtained if the tank is served by a 2½ inch (62 mm) or 3 inch (75 mm) rainwater pipe. An overflow pipe is essential; it should never be less than 2 inches (50 mm) in diameter and should be brought down to a surface channel or rainwater gully. The tank should be set on brick supports in such a way that there is a slight fall-away from the wall. An inconspicuous position should, of course, be chosen and it may well be desirable to screen it with shrubs.

Rubbish is often allowed to accumulate for far too long. It should be collected in a clearly identifiable spot, away from the church and well screened from view. Dead flowers and grass-clippings should be separately provided for, on a compost heap in a screened-off corner of the churchyard: the compost can then be used on any flower beds the churchyard may have. Other rubbish should be burned at frequent intervals and on a day when the wind is blowing away from the church. Bonfires should not be lit on, around, or near memorials. An incinerator may be required for the burning of wreaths. (Sometimes these are almost incombustible.) It is illegal to light an open fire within 50 feet (15 metres) of the public highway.

LIGHTING AND NOTICE-BOARDS

The approach to a church may be made or marred by its notice-board or the churchyard lighting. These details are of such importance that they should be a matter for careful consideration in association with the church architect. The overall impact of church and churchyard needs always to be borne in mind.

Artificial lighting in the churchyard should be provided in a simple but attractive form. A plain lantern or a wall light on an oak post can be placed to light the pathway. Lights should not be fixed to the outside walls of churches or, generally, to a lych-gate; but if, because of wanton damage, a more substantial type of fitting is necessary, bulkhead lights may be erected, provided they are strongly fixed to the wall. Concrete lamp posts of most of the standard municipal types should be scrupulously avoided. The best examples of currently available mass-produced lamp standards may be studied in the collection displayed at the Design Centre, 28 Haymarket, London SW1.

Old lamp frames over gates can be easily adapted to modern purposes and safety conditions, but this should be done *only* by a professional electrician. All new outdoor light-fittings should be of non-ferrous metal to avoid rusting.

Great care needs to be taken about the flood-lighting of a church. No building was built to be illuminated from the ground – or from within – and it is often better to have lamps shining from an adjoining building. On the other hand, it is important that a flood-lighting scheme should take into account the relationship of the church with other buildings. Sometimes only certain features, such as the spire or tower, should be flood-lit. Good flood-lighting should suggest moonlight rather than the harsh glare of a shopping precinct. In every case, the church architect should be consulted. It may be wise to illuminate a building only for certain occasions rather than to install a system permanently.

Separate church notice-boards are often considered unnecessary; in the country it is often thought sufficient to exhibit notices in the church porch. The provision of adequate and accessible notice-boards is especially important, however, in united benefices or grouped parishes, where the services may be at a variety of times. A notice giving 'Times of services' might also be exhibited elsewhere in the village – near the inn, the shop or the bus stop. Because of the increase in vandalism and thefts, many churches have to be kept locked, and this at a time when more and more visitors are – happily – genuinely anxious to see inside them. Accessibility is a condition of English Heritage grants; moreover the ready availability of a key may be a vital factor in case of fire. A locked church, with no notice of welcome or indication of the availability of a key, conveys a distinctly negative impression. It is, therefore, from every point of view vital that a notice in the porch should indicate where a key may be obtained and preferably give several alternatives.

In the case of urban churches it is probably sufficient to erect one good free-standing notice-board close to the main entrance gates; and it is helpful if the notice-board can be sited fairly near a lamp post so that it can be seen at night. It is better to avoid siting notice-boards under trees but, if this is unavoidable, then it is sensible to protect them by providing for a projecting top-moulding, with a covering such as bituminous felt or lead. The supporting posts should be painted with two coats of paint.

Black letters on a white or cream-coloured background, or white on a background of dark blue, red, dark green or black show up well. The example of the National Trust is well worth studying, as their notices are excellent. Gold letters on unpainted wood, or incised letters, though attractive in themselves, are not so easily read.

It is worth taking a good deal of trouble over every aspect of the notice-board, both in terms of its design and in terms of the information it is intended to convey. In many cases, particularly in the country, all that is needed is the name and dedication of the church (it is important to identify the church readily in that way), the address and telephone number of the parish priest and perhaps also one other point of contact (e.g. a churchwarden), and – if they do not vary too much – the times of the regular services. Generally speaking, the briefer the wording, the more effective the message.

The design for a permanent notice-board should be referred to the Diocesan Advisory Committee for advice, and be carried out by a professional (or really good amateur) sign-writer or lettering artist. A sloppy or amateurish notice-board is a powerful disincentive.

The legal requirements regarding notice-boards are given elsewhere, but in any case they are subject to standard conditions requiring them to be kept clean and tidy. Informal enquiry of the local planning authority's staff may be both helpful and sensible. In a Conservation Area the advice of the Conservation Officer might well be sought, as on many other matters respecting the environmental and wider aspects of the care of church and churchyard.

DRAINAGE

The drainage of the churchyard may be vital to the maintenance of the church building, especially in cases where the flooding of boiler houses or burial vaults is experienced or where the church obstructs the natural disposal of surface water from a steeply sloping site; still more important is adequate provision for the drainage of rainwater discharged from the roofs by means of proper soakaways and land drains. Disposal from the church roof may be by gutters and downpipes, from overhanging eaves or by means of projecting rainwater spouts. In the first method it is essential that the concentrated rainwater discharge should be quickly and effectively dispersed through surface channels or gullies and underground drainpipes to soakaways or ditches. Where roofs drain by means of overhanging eaves, a perimeter channel linked to underground drains or, alternatively, a subsoil with good drainage properties is essential if the wall footings are not to become saturated. Where spouts are used, carefully sited catchment areas, again linked to underground drains, are necessary, especially where the absorption-quality of the subsoil is poor.

As historic churches were constructed without damp-proof courses they are invariably by modern standards damp and, where the wall core is of loosely constituted rubble of some thickness, poorly suited to proprietary damp-proofing techniques. This is not necessarily the disadvantage it was once supposed, provided the interior wall finishes, panelling and floor surfaces are designed to perform in above-average moisture conditions and to facilitate the evaporation of dampness absorbed from the soil outside.

Unnecessary damage is on occasion caused by the construction of drainage trenches at wall bases where the ground level of the churchyard is higher than that of the floor within. Such trenches can undermine the shallow wall-footings of medieval buildings, expose the supporting subsoil to frost attack, and destroy important archaeological material. Provided gutters, downpipes, gullies and drains are not leaking or blocked (nine out of ten cases of severe damp damage are due to gutter and gully defects), it is generally possible to keep rising damp at an acceptable level without recourse to exterior trenching.

In cases where an existing ground drainage system is functioning imperfectly or has become blocked, cleaning and repairs should always be attempted initially. Where repairs are not possible or seem to be ineffective, expert advice should automatically be sought before radical changes are contemplated, let alone enacted. Drainage improvements, in common with all alterations to church buildings, require faculty consent, as does any disturbance of human remains, which frequently lie buried at shallow levels in unmarked positions beneath the surface of the churchyard.

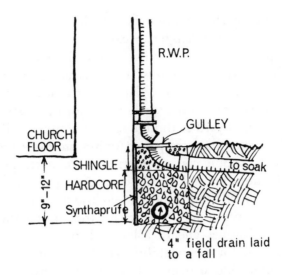

This drawing shows the construction of a 'French' drain, which can sometimes be an appropriate solution for damp church walls. In addition to the structural problems which need to be taken into account, this is also the most sensitive area archaeologically, and special care needs to be taken when such a drain is laid.

Prevention, however, is better than cure. It is good practice to walk round the church every week to ensure that gullies and channels are clear of dead leaves. Watch for flooding and blocked drains after heavy rain. Lift manhole covers and rod drains annually. Make a map of the drains surrounding the church and hang a copy in the vestry. Fasten another in the front of the fabric maintenance log book. Vigilance costs nothing and can literally save money being poured down the drain.

ALTERATIONS TO EXISTING CHURCHYARDS

By its very nature, a churchyard eventually becomes filled with graves, and a decision may need to be taken with regard to making some changes or providing an extension. The fashion for 're-ordering' churchyards has now abated, and a more conservative approach is generally favoured. 'Tidiness' is now no longer regarded as being next to godliness.

Gravestones, kerbs and mounds have all at times been regarded as obstacles to the easy maintenance of the churchyard grass. Any proposals put forward for their removal or re-arrangement require careful scrutiny and must never detract from the essential character of a churchyard as the place of burial near a church. This character, as we have said elsewhere, is not best maintained by treating the churchyard as though it were a municipal garden or park. At the earliest stage the parish (or in some cases it may be the local authority) should consult the church architect, the Diocesan Advisory Committee and the Diocesan Archaeological Adviser, for advice on which tombstones should in any event be retained *in situ*. The presumption should be, in fact, that most of them will be retained – kerbstones and to a lesser degree mounds are in a different category of expendability. The Diocesan Archaeological Adviser will be able to help with the deciphering of apparently illegible inscriptions, and give advice on all aspects of recording the churchyard and its memorials. It may also be necessary to arrange for the lifting and refixing of sunken gravestones, so that they will be more visible and less of a hazard. Table tombs may require repointing or other repairs. Many important memorials may now be 'listed'. The Diocesan Registrar should be contacted at the same time as advice is sought from the Diocesan Advisory Committee, so that the legal procedures can be clarified and put in hand.

Any scheme which involves the wholesale removal or substantial repair of stones or kerbs or mounds is a matter for an application for faculty. The value of this statutory protection is particularly apparent in such a situation. It allows a parish some freedom of action, while at the same time enabling interested parties to state their case; and it inhibits the wholesale or thoughtless destruction of valuable historical evidence.

Generally speaking, there will be no objection to the complete removal of kerbs or mounds, or to the removal of totally illegible and irreparably damaged stones. It should be remembered, though, that what will appear illegible to most people will not necessarily be illegible to the expert, and the recording of gravestones and their inscriptions demands expert attention. Kerbs may be sunk or laid level with the turf, or preferably

Plate 12. *The products of the Compton Pottery, at Compton in Surrey were used even for headstones, as well as for the spectacular mausoleum.*

Plate 13. *Thursley, Surrey: a revival of the use of a wooden 'leaping board', with a beautiful verse.*

Plate 14. *Hexton, Hertfordshire: An eighteenth-century 'leaping board' survives the rigours of the English climate.*

IF I TAKE THE WINGS
OF THE MORNING
AND REMAIN IN THE
UTTERMOST PARTS
OF THE SEA;
EVEN THERE ALSO
SHALL THY HAND
LEAD ME, AND THY
RIGHT HAND SHALL
HOLD ME.

Plate 15. *Busbridge, Surrey: a noble design in oak, now some 60 years old and weathered to a silver-grey colour.*

Plate 16. *St Enedoc, Trebetherick, Cornwall: Simon Verity's spectacular headstone evokes the many-talented personality of the late Poet Laureate, John Betjeman.*

Plate 17. *Burford, Oxfordshire: an unusually elaborate cast iron grave-marker.*

Plate 19.   Little Barrington, Gloucestershire: the conservators Sue and Lawrence Kelland have dismantled and re-erected two important monuments, using soft lime mortar and non-ferrous metal cramps.

removed altogether. If there are inscriptions on the kerb the face can be turned so that the words are still readable. The simplest method is to dig a trench alongside and turn the kerb into its own 'grave'. Mounds must be treated with respect; they were once the marker for the poor man's grave. Therefore it is all the more important that specific mention is included in the faculty application. If permission is given for their removal, mounds can best be levelled by a straight incision up the centre and the earth removed from under the turf. Alternatively, soil from other graves can be put alongside to build up the level. Prevention is better than cure and in filling a new grave not all the excavated earth on top of the grave need be replaced. The majority of illegible or seriously damaged stones can be removed altogether; but care should be taken when any are of aesthetic, historical or genealogical value. They may also be protecting other and exceptionally interesting gravestones from more severe weathering. Certain wrought-iron railings and chains are also of value and the Diocesan Advisory Committee's advice should be sought before considering their removal.

Any scheme for the re-arrangement of gravestones will depend upon the purpose of the exercise. In all cases where the churchyard forms a setting for the church, the preservation of the churchyard's character as a church burial ground should be kept in mind, and many if not all the older stones should be preserved *in situ*. If the primary purpose is to release an area of the churchyard for reburial, then some stones can be re-aligned or their position altered to enable new graves to be dug. Such a scheme means that an area need not be cleared all at once but can be prepared as the space is required. In that case, particular thought needs to be given to the type and material of the new monuments which should be permitted amongst the older stones.

If the scheme is primarily to make it easier to use mechanical implements for regular maintenance work, then the re-arrangement must be planned to permit their easy use and manoeuvring. The scale of a churchyard normally requires the mechanical implement to be guided by a man on foot: a tractor will in most cases be over-large and inappropriate.

Sometimes the drawing-up of a scheme is taken as the

opportunity for weeding out some of the more glaring and inharmonious tombstones such as those made of white marble or black granite in a churchyard where natural stone of sympathetic colour is otherwise extensively used. At the same time, less aesthetically satisfying designs (e.g. bird-baths and the like) could be moved to some less obtrusive part of the churchyard. Generally, tombstones which are moved for the sake of easier maintenance should be reinstated as near as possible to their original positions.

The Commonwealth War Graves Commission has had the unfortunate experience of headstones being removed from Commonwealth war graves without any prior notification to the Commission. This is untenable, and it is most important to ensure that if any tentative proposals are envisaged which involve Commonwealth war graves or headstones, the Commission should be informed at once through the Diocesan Registrar. Headstones which are the responsibility of the Commission are not necessarily of the standard type and may not therefore be readily recognisable, and it is therefore advisable that the Commission should be notified as a matter of courtesy in *all* cases where a faculty application involves removal of headstones.

The simplest re-arrangement of stones is to re-arrange them in parallel rows, but this is totally to destroy the churchyard pattern and the whole significance of the stones as 'grave markers'. Where a larger area of cut grass is required, some tombstones could perhaps be arranged in short lines parallel to the churchyard wall and set in gravel so that weeds can be easily contained. *The general rule is that the minimum number of stones should be moved from their original position.* In parts of Lancashire or Yorkshire (e.g. the churchyards of St John and St Peter in the heart of Leeds) there is an ancient and local tradition of placing gravestones level with the ground, but aside from such local traditions, the effect of producing a virtually paved area and the removal of every vertical scale in a churchyard can be disastrous. Moreover, tombstones should never be laid beside or stacked against a churchyard wall like a pack of cards. If you are unfortunate enough to have inherited a churchyard where this has happened, consideration should be given to restoring them to their rightful place.

Only completely decayed stones should be broken up and buried in the churchyard. The greatest scandal can be, and regrettably has been, caused by the sale of such stones or by deliberate defacement or damage. Do not 'mark' memorials with any type of paint.

SUGGESTED PROCEDURE

Each churchyard is individual and demands individual treatment. In addition to seeking advice from outside the parish, e.g. from the Diocesan Advisory Committee, the Diocesan Archaeological Adviser, the inspecting architect or an experienced landscape architect, the congregation should itself be asked for ideas and suggestions. Tentative proposals should be very fully explained, and comments or suggestions invited, in the parish magazine and perhaps also at a well-organised parish meeting with proper explanatory material. Someone from the Diocesan Advisory Committee or the local history society might be asked to take parishioners on a 'churchyard walk', pointing out the different styles, the meaning of the symbolism, and the historical content of the inscriptions. Interest may be aroused in local schools, leading to the school-children making a survey of the churchyard and producing a report on their findings. Oxford University Press have published a pamphlet on this subject for use in schools, in their Schools Council Integrated Studies series.

No action should be taken until all ideas have been considered and the best solution for your particular churchyard decided upon. You may indeed find that no change is the best solution. What is right for a neighbouring churchyard will almost certainly not be right for yours – although it is useful to see what has been done elsewhere, even if only to see how not to do it. The test is both to ensure that nothing is destroyed which ought to be preserved and that the setting of the church should still be appropriate. In the Herefordshire volume in the Buildings of England series, Sir Nikolaus Pevsner pinpointed exactly what ought not to happen in the case of one important church (Leominster Priory):

> The church today stands, pale red on juicy green, in a curious isolation surrounded on three sides by lawn (and the churchyard), and these lawns and open spaces stretch quite a distance to the south. The building looks

thus neither like a priory church nor like a parish church. One is almost reminded of a model,

To sum up, all monuments or fragments earlier than the early nineteenth century should be kept, virtually without exception. Every churchyard monument of the seventeenth and eighteenth centuries is likely to be of good design and craftsmanship, and equally will be of genealogical interest to historians and demographers. Tombstones of this period should only be destroyed if past all repair. Nineteenth-century monuments may generally also be worth preserving, both for intrinsic merit and for genealogical or historical interest. If the churchyard is overcrowded, untidy and difficult to mow, some modest degree of partial clearance may be desirable, but it is unnecessary elements like kerbs, bird-baths and vases which should be reviewed first; then, if still more room for manoeuvre is required, stones which have become featureless or illegible or broken beyond repair might be considered. The object should be to obtain enough leeway in which to use a mower and to free the walls of the church from obstructions, not to release space for ambitious gardening. Every effort should be made not to change radically the appearance and character of the churchyard.

The following procedure is recommended:

1. To prepare a numbered plan and a register of graves with a copy in full of each monumental inscription. The recording of the inscriptions should be carried out by someone with a proper interest and the necessary expertise. Recording the appearance of gravestones and their carvings and inscriptions by means of photographs, slides and drawings is also desirable.

2. To consult the Diocesan Advisory Committee and the Diocesan Archaeological Adviser, who will advise upon monuments of outstanding merit that ought to be preserved. A delegation or representative of the DAC will usually make a visit of inspection before the advice can be given. Contact should at this stage also be made with the Diocesan Registrar.

3. After consultation with the Diocesan Advisory Committee (and, if so advised, with the inspecting architect), to list the tombstones which it is desired to clear and to decide, again with

the advice of the Diocesan Advisory Committee, what to do with them.

4. To apply for a faculty, by which time the Registrar will have advised what should be done about consulting the relatives or representatives of any persons whose tombstones are to be displaced, if they are of recent date. Active efforts have to be made to trace relatives, in order to comply with the Faculty Jurisdiction Measure 1964; advertising may not be enough.

5. Subject to the advice of the Registrar, to advertise the proposal in the local press and in the parish magazine, inviting objectors, if any, to come forward by a certain date. (This is a legal requirement, but in fact it is still more desirable that any proposal involving alterations to a churchyard should be the subject of a sympathetic and informative article in the local newspaper which will explain to the interested public at large what is intended.) Untold pastoral harm can be done by schemes of alteration or 'improvement' to churchyards without proper study of what exists and what ought to be retained, and without full and careful (and open-minded) consultation and explanation. The effort expended in all these directions will be richly repaid.

Appendices

Appendices

Suggested Rules to Govern the Introduction of Churchyard Memorials and the Care and Maintenance of Churchyards

EXPLANATION

Incumbents and PCCs should study this explanation and Chapters 5, 6 and 7 of this Handbook carefully before they formulate their own churchyard rules.

Faculties are normally required for any work undertaken in churches or churchyards, including the introduction of memorials to commemorate the departed. However, many diocesan Chancellors have delegated authority to incumbents permitting them to allow simple headstones which fall within the terms and conditions of the delegation. Such delegations are often referred to as 'diocesan churchyard regulations', but their function is primarily to define the extent of the authority which the incumbent can exercise without reference to the Chancellor.

If a proposed memorial falls outside the scope of the delegation the applicant still has the right to petition the Chancellor for a faculty. Where an applicant wishes to erect a memorial which differs from the normal standards indicated in these Rules, but which appears to be of good design, the incumbent should encourage the proposal to be sent forward to the Chancellor for a faculty.

During a vacancy, and thus where there is no incumbent, and also where there is a priest-in-charge, the Chancellor's authority is delegated to the Rural Dean and it is important to remember that it is exercisable only by him.

It is thought that these suggested rules may be of assistance to Chancellors in formulating their delegated authority, and also for use by PCCs. It is essential that before PCCs make their own rules they should consult the Diocesan Registrar to ensure that they will be compatible with the Chancellor's directions.

SUGGESTED RULES

1 *Procedure for the Introduction of Memorials*

Permission must be obtained for the introduction of any memorial. Simple upright grave markers in respect of burials may be authorised by the incumbent in accordance with the terms and conditions given below; but other types of memorial, including grave markers such as horizontal ledgers, sculpture and crosses, must be authorised by the Chancellor under faculty. Applications for specially designed and appropriate memorials will be sympathetically considered by the Chancellor.

Every application to erect a memorial, or place anything whatsoever, or to do any works, in the churchyard should be made in writing to the incumbent, in the first instance, with a full description of the proposed work. Applications for the introduction of memorials should be made on the form issued by the diocese and obtainable from the incumbent in writing. Permission to erect a memorial must be obtained from the incumbent before accepting an estimate or otherwise entering into a contract with a funeral director or stonemason. A minimum period of six months must elapse between the death of a person to be commemorated and the approval of a memorial by the incumbent [exercising his delegated authority].

2 *Dimensions of Headstone*

Headstones should be no larger than 120mm (4ft) high, measured from the surface of the ground, 900mm (3ft) wide and 150mm (6in) thick. They should be no less than 750mm (2ft 6in) high, 500mm (1ft 8in) wide and no less than 75mm (3in) thick (except in the case of slate memorials, which may be thinner but no less than 38mm (1½in thick.) These measurements are not intended to define standard proportions of memorials, and memorials may be of any dimensions within the given maxima and minima. (The metric equivalents given above are slightly less than the Imperial dimensions, but are recommended for use by the National Association of Master Masons.)

3 *Base and Foundation Slab*

A headstone may stand on a stone base, provided that it is an integral part of the design and does not project more than 102mm (4in) beyond the headstone in any direction, except where a receptacle for flowers is provided, in which case this should be flush with the top of the base and may extend up to 200mm (8in) in front of the headstone. Due regard should be paid to the nature of the ground and the problem of settlement.

Other methods of fixing the memorial in the ground are not discouraged, and the base of the memorial may be so shaped that it can be inserted directly into the ground at sufficient depth to ensure stability.

4   Materials

All memorials should be made of natural stone with no reflecting finish, or of hardwood. Stones traditionally used in local buildings, or stones closely similar to them in colour and texture, are to be preferred. Black, blue or red granites are not permitted under these terms and conditions, nor granites darker than Rustenburg grey, nor white marble, synthetic stone or plastic.

5   Sculpture

Figure sculpture and other statuary are not discouraged, but must be authorised by faculty.

6   Designs

Headstones need not be restricted to a rectangular shape, and curved tops are preferable to straight-edged ones. Memorials in the shape of a heart or book are not permitted other than by faculty, nor are photographs, porcelain portraits, kerbs, railings, chains, chippings or glass shades.

Graves of the Commonwealth War Graves Commission: Gravestones provided by the Commonwealth War Graves are of distinctive design and dimensions to indicate their special nature. The standard dimensions are 2ft 8in high and 1ft 3in broad. These are without the standards normally approved above but are permitted without the need for a faculty. Special care may be required in locating such stones so that their distinctive appearance does not conflict with older memorials of different proportions.

7   Epitaphs

Inscriptions must be simple and reverent, and may include felicitous quotations from literary sources. Inscriptions should be incised, or in relief, and may be painted. Plastic or other inserted lettering should not be permitted. Additions may be made to an inscription at a later date following a subsequent interment in the same grave or for other suitable reason. However, any such alteration must be separately approved. The lettering, lay-out and wording must be consistent with the original inscription.

8 Trademarks

No advertisement or trademark should be inscribed on a headstone. The mason's name may be inscribed at the side or on the reverse in unleaded letters, no larger than 13mm (½in) in height.

9 Commemoration after Cremation

The erection of a memorial tablet is not permitted except in areas set aside by faculty, and then only in accordance with the terms of the faculty. However, a suitable addition to an existing memorial stone relating to a close relative may be permitted. Commemoration in a Book of Remembrance is preferable to commemoration by an individual memorial stone.

10 Flowers

Except where the design of a headstone includes an integral receptacle for plants or cut flowers, they may be placed in a removable container, which must be sunk completely into the ground.

Wreaths and cut flowers may be placed in such containers or laid on any grave, but must be removed as soon as they appear to be withered. No artificial flowers should be allowed except for Remembrance Day poppies and traditional Christmas wreaths and these should be removed after a period of not more than two months. Bulbs may be planted in the soil of any grave.

11 Churchyard Maintenance

The surface of the churchyard will be kept free from grave mounds and as level as possible, so that the grass may be easily cut by a mower.

APPENDIX II

A Suggested Procedure for Care of the Churchyard

(1) The parochial church council (the PCC) should adopt by formal resolution a set of rules covering the use and maintenance of the churchyard, following the lines of those given in Appendix I and with particular reference to any rules or regulations which may have been laid down by the Chancellor of the diocese.

(2) A framed copy of these rules should be displayed in the church porch, together with an indication that:

(a) Advice about suitable stones, appropriate design and the composition of inscriptions may be obtained from the incumbent (or some other person).

(b) Before permission is given to a stonemason to begin work on any memorial, the design, with the inscription properly set out in the style of lettering to be used and with full particulars of the material, dimensions and proposed foundation work for setting up the stone, must be submitted to the incumbent for his approval, which must be obtained in writing.

(c) Before beginning work the mason must show that he is adequately covered by insurance.

(3) The rules, and a copy of the resolution of the PCC covering their adoption, should be sent to local monumental masons and funeral directors; they should also be individually informed of the necessity of obtaining the incumbent's approval in writing.

(4) An account should be established for the maintenance of the churchyard and the money deposited. Bequests of £50 or £100 or more should be invited, through the parish magazine or the local press, from all who expect to be buried in the churchyard. A collecting plate labelled

'Churchyard Maintenance Fund' might be placed near the church door at funerals, and a special house-to-house collection made at All Saints' tide. (For a house-to-house collection permission is required from the District Council.)

(5) A member of the PCC with a small committee might be appointed to administer this fund and relieve the incumbent of responsibility. If the local authority contributes towards the maintenance of the churchyard (see Chapter 8), one or two of its members might be co-opted to this committee. In addition to the PCC and the local authority, it is important to establish a working partnership with the actual facilities directly concerned, such as monumental masons and funeral directors, and to harness the voluntary help of a cross-section of the parish.

(6) A successful scheme has been in operation over a considerable period at Penn, in Buckinghamshire, and the special committee established here is called the Churchyard Guild, much of the detailed administrative work and correspondence with the next of kin being delegated to its secretary.

(7) If a fund is established for churchyard maintenance, the PCC should establish a Trust Deed in association with the Diocesan Board of Finance, so that capital monies for long-term upkeep can be lodged for investment (see Appendix III). The Investment Fund of the Central Board of Finance of the Church of England is a suitable medium, and the interest can now be paid quarterly. In addition, the PCC should open a special churchyard fund account, and arrange with the bank that the outstanding balance at the end of each month shall be transferred automatically into their general account. This avoids the need for a separate treasurer, as all outgoings are thereby made through the PCC treasurer, following the advice and directions of the incumbent and guild secretary.

(8) A scale of standard annual contributions towards the upkeep of the churchyard generally should be fixed by the PCC, e.g. £10 p.a. (which would be approximately 10p per week for grave maintenance and 10p for general churchyard upkeep and capital costs). The use of banker's order forms and deeds of covenant should be encouraged.

(9) The incumbent should invite the churchyard guild or committee to share in the work generally, and its members should cover a wide cross-section of the parish as a whole. They can help provide continuity of policy over a period of years. From time to time, working parties of men, women and children too, should be encouraged, the object being to involve as many individuals as possible.

(10) A plan of the churchyard drawn to scale and showing the whereabouts of individual graves is an essential requirement. Each grave should be given a number in its plot or section (see Chapter 16, Recording the Churchyard).

(11) A comprehensive card index recording all burials and memorials is also desirable, both for present usage and for future reference. Each card should ideally show date of death, age, date of funeral, burial register number, names and addresses of next of kin and their relationship, type of memorial, plot and grave numbers; also names and addresses of the family solicitors, bankers and executors, to enable contact to be maintained over the long term. Obviously such records would include a note as to whether a family made their contributions through an annual subscription, banker's order, deed of covenant or lump sum.

Model Advertisement of Proposed Alteration(s) to a Churchyard

Proposed alteration(s) to the churchyard of (a) ....
at (b) ....
TAKE NOTICE that petition is being made by (c) ....
incumbent of the Parish of (a) .... and (d) ....
of .... and (d) .... of ....
churchwardens of that parish, to The Chancellor of the Diocese of
(e) ....
for a faculty to carry out the following alteration(s) to the above
churchyard namely:–
(f) ....
....
....

A copy of the petition and of all plans and other documents relating
thereto may be inspected by interested parties at (g) ....
....
at all reasonable hours until (h) ....
....
Any person who wishes to make representations about the matter should
make them in writing by that date to (i) ....
....

	Signed	....
★	On behalf of	....
	Date	....

★ Delete where inappropriate
(a) Insert name of parish
(b) Insert location of churchyard
(c) Insert name of incumbent
(d) Insert names and addresses of churchwardens
(e) Insert name of diocese
(f) Insert description of proposed alteration(s)
(g) Insert address of Diocesan Registrar or such other place as the Registrar may direct
(h) Insert date not less than 3 months later than the date on which the notice is posted
(i) Insert name and address of Diocesan Registrar.

Model Application Form to Incumbent to Introduce a Memorial into a Churchyard or to Amend an Inscription

Diocese of

APPLICATION

BY   DATE

OF

FOR PERMISSION TO ERECT (or add to inscription on) MEMORIAL

AT CHURCHYARD OF   GRAVE NO.

GRAVE OF

DETAILS OF PROPOSAL
(Give dimensional sketch over page)

MATERIAL   COLOUR

FINISH

OVERALL SIZES (height first)

PROPOSED INSCRIPTION(S)

APPROVED   DATE   FEES £

Model Trust Deed for the Upkeep of Graves

THIS DEED is made the .... day of .... One thousand nine hundred and .... BETWEEN THE PAROCHIAL CHURCH COUNCIL OF .... in the Diocese of .... (hereinafter called 'the PCC') of the one part and THE .... DIOCESAN BOARD OF FINANCE incorporated under the Companies Acts not for profit whose registered office is situate at Diocesan Church House (hereinafter called 'the Board') of the other part

WHEREAS the PCC has recently paid to the Board a sum of .... pounds to be invested and held by the Board upon the trusts and with and subject to the powers and provisions hereinafter specified and declared of and concerning the same which said sum of .... pounds TOGETHER WITH all gifts legacies bequests and donations whether money or other property received by the PCC or the Board as an addition thereto and the investments from time to time representing the same are hereinafter referred to as 'the Trust Fund'

AND WHEREAS it has been agreed that the management of the trust shall be vested in the PCC as Administrative Trustees so long as the PCC are entitled to the income thereof

NOW THIS DEED WITNESSETH AND IT IS HEREBY AGREED AND DECLARED as follows:
1. THE Board shall stand possessed of the Trust Fund upon the trusts and for the charitable ecclesiastical purposes hereinafter provided
2. THE Board shall pay the income of the Trust Fund to the PCC to be applied by the PCC for the purposes and in the manner hereinafter provided so long as the PCC is entitled to receive the same
3. THE income of the Trust Fund shall be applied by the PCC for the general upkeep of the Churchyard and the Church of .... in the said Parish.
4. PROVIDED ALWAYS that in so far as any part of the Trust Fund has been or shall be contributed subject to a condition that a particular grave situate in the said Churchyard is kept in clean and proper order and condition then if for a period of twelve consecutive months such grave is not kept the capital sum whether money or securities representing such

part of the Trust Fund shall be held for the Board absolutely to be applied in or towards carrying on the charitable objects of the Board or any of them

5. A Certificate signed when required by the Rural Dean that any grave is maintained in clean and proper order and condition shall be sufficient evidence in that behalf and any question as to the breach of the requirements that any grave shall be so kept shall be finally settled by him

6. THE receipt of the Treasurer of the PCC for any income paid over to the PCC by the Board shall be a sufficient discharge to the Board for the same

7. THE Board may at any time instead of paying the said income to the PCC permit the PCC to receive the same or may pay or cause the same to be paid into the banking account of the PCC to be applied in the same manner as if it had been paid to the PCC and any such receipt by permission or by payment into the said banking account shall discharge the Board from the same and the Board shall under no circumstances be liable or responsible to see to the application of any moneys paid to or received by the PCC or paid into such account as aforesaid or for the acts or defaults of any bank with which any such banking account as aforesaid shall be kept

8. THE Board may invest the Trust Fund or any part thereof in or upon such shares stocks funds securities or other investments in any part of the world as the Board shall in its absolute discretion think fit and so that the Board shall be empowered to invest vary and transpose the investment of trust moneys in the same unrestricted manner as if it were the beneficiary or entitled to all such moneys

IN WITNESS whereof the Chairman and two other members of the PCC on behalf of the PCC have hereunto set their respective hands and seals and the Board has caused its Corporate Seal to be hereunto affixed the day and year first before written

SIGNED SEALED AND DELIVERED by
 being the Chairman and
 and
being two other members of the Council on
behalf of the PCC in the presence of:

THE CORPORATE SEAL OF THE
DIOCESAN BOARD OF FINANCE was
hereunto affixed in the presence of:

Members

Secretary

Model Form of Receipt for a Gift

inter vivos

for Upkeep of Graves

(for use by Diocesan Boards of Finance)

THE DIOCESAN BOARD OF FINANCE of the Diocese of ....
HEREBY ACKNOWLEDGES the receipt of £...............★★...............
from .... to be held upon trust to pay the income to the
(Parochial Church Council) (Incumbent) of the Parish of
.... in the County of .... and the Diocese
of .... for the maintenance of the church and churchyard
of the said Parish so long as the grave of .... in such
churchyard is kept in good order and repair. From and after any breach of
this condition coming to their knowledge the said Board shall hold the
said sum and the investments representing the same and the income
thereof for the general purposes of the Board. A Certificate signed every
three years by the Rural Dean that the said grave is so kept shall be
sufficient evidence in that behalf and any question as to breach of this
condition shall be finally settled by him.

★★ The sum of money should provide an income amply sufficient to keep the
grave in order, so as to enable the condition of the trust to be fulfilled without
difficulty.

Note: Gifts in this form or under form (e) create valid charitable trusts subject to a
condition (upkeep of a specified grave) which is not charitable, and to pass a gift
over in the event of a breach of that condition. Money spent on maintenance of a
grave is not applied for charitable purposes. It is important therefore that the
whole of the trust income be applied for the maintenance of the churchyard as a
whole and that the specified grave be maintained in repair from other sources in
the hands of the recipient of the trust income.

Model Form of a Receipt for a Gift
inter vivos
for Upkeep of Graves in Perpetuity
(for use by PCCs)

THE PAROCHIAL CHURCH COUNCIL (PCC) of the Parish of
.... in the Diocese of .... HEREBY
ACKNOWLEDGES the receipt of .... from
.... to be applied by the said PCC upon the Trusts of a
Deed of Declaration of Trust for the upkeep of the Churchyard of the
Church of .... dated the .... day of
.... and made between the said PCC of the one part and
The .... Diocesan Board of Finance of the other part and
the said PCC FURTHER ACKNOWLEDGES that the Proviso in
Clause 4 of the said Declaration of Trust shall apply in relation to the
grave of .... in the said Churchyard.

DATED THE .... day of ....

Treasurer of the Parochial
Church Council

Note: See note to form (d)

Model Form of Legacy for Upkeep of Graves

I GIVE THE SUM OF £............ free of Inheritance Tax to the .... Diocesan Board of Finance Upon Trust to pay the income to the (Parochial Church Council) (Incumbent) of the Parish of .... in the County of .... and Diocese of .... for the maintenance of the church and churchyard of the said Parish so long as the grave of .... in such a churchyard is kept in good order and repair. From and after any breach of this condition coming to the knowledge of the said Board I direct that the said Board shall hold the said sum and the investments representing the same and the income thereof for the general purposes of the Board. A certificate signed every three years by the Rural Dean that the said grave is so kept shall be sufficient evidence in that behalf and any question as to breach of this condition shall be finally settled by him.

Note: Legacies must be included in a will or a codicil to a will which has been drawn up and executed in accordance with the normal legal requirements.

Model Agreement for Contributions by a Local Authority Towards the Expenses of Maintaining a Closed Churchyard

THIS AGREEMENT is made the .... day of .... 19 ....
BETWEEN the .... (a) Council (hereinafter called the
.... (b) Council) of the one part and the Parochial Church
Council of the Parish of .... (c) (hereinafter called the PCC)
of the other part

WHEREAS

(1) The churchyard of the parish church of .... is nearly
full and it is generally agreed that the most suitable mode of providing
further burial space for the inhabitants of the parish would be by an
addition to the churchyard.

(2) The PCC have agreed to take all necessary steps to secure an
addition of approximately .... square metres in consideration of
the .... (b) Council undertaking to make an annual
contribution towards the maintenance of the whole of the churchyard in
pursuance of their powers under section 214 of the Local Government
Act 1972.

NOW IT IS HEREBY AGREED as follows:

1. The .... (b) Council undertake to pay the sum of
£................ to the PCC annually on the .... day of .... in each
year for the next ten years [and thereafter until such time as this
agreement is terminated by not less than six months' notice].

2. The PCC undertakes to use the said sum of £................ exclusively
towards the expenses incurred by them in maintaining the churchyard
(including any addition thereto) as a place of interment in which the
remains of the inhabitants of the parish are or may be interred.

As witness etc.

[Signatures on behalf of parties]

(a) Insert name of local authority
(b) Give abbreviation for the local authority
(c) Insert name of parish

Alternative Model Agreement for Contributions by a Local Authority towards the Expenses of Maintaining a Churchyard

THIS AGREEMENT is made the .... day of .... 19........ BETWEEN the .... (a) (hereinafter called the .... (b) Council) of the one part and the Parochial Church Council of the Parish of .... (c) (hereinafter called the PCC) of the other part.

WHEREAS

(1) In addition to the churchyard belonging to the parish church most of the other places of worship in the area of the .... (b) Council have burial grounds attached to them and therefore it has not been necessary for the .... (b) Council to provide a burial ground or cemetery for their area.

(2) In view of the increased cost of maintaining the parish churchyard the PCC requested the .... (b) Council to seek powers to contribute regularly towards such expenses, which the .... (b) Council agreed to do.

(3) The .... (b) Council have obtained an order from the Secretary of State for the Department of the Environment [or the Secretary of State for Wales] under section 251 of the Local Government Act 1972 giving the .... (b) Council the powers of a parish council under section 10 of the Parish Council Act 1957.

NOW IT IS HEREBY AGREED as follows:

1. The .... (b) Council undertake to pay the sum of £ .... to the PCC annually on the .... day of .... in each year until such time as this agreement is terminated on not less than six months' notice.

2. The PCC undertake to use the said sum of £ .... exclusively towards the expenses incurred by them in maintaining their churchyard as a place of interment in which the remains of the inhabitants of the .... (b) Council area are or may be interred.

AS WITNESS etc.

[Signatures on behalf of parties]

(a)   Insert name of local authority
(b)   Give abbreviation for the local authority
(a)   Insert name of the Parish

Model Terms of Agreement for Requiring Provision of Insurance Cover in Respect of Work on Monuments in Churchyards

THIS AGREEMENT is made the .... day of .... 19 .... BETWEEN the incumbent, and the Parochial Church Council of the Parish of .... (a) .... (hereinafter called 'the PCC') on the one part, and .... (b) .... of .... (hereinafter called 'the Contractor'), on the other part.

1. Subject to this agreement, the Contractor is authorised to carry out the following work in the churchyard of the said Parish, at .... (c) .... namely .... (d) ....

2. In consideration of the Contractor being authorised to carry out such work in the said churchyard, the Contractor undertakes that he will, unless already covered by an appropriate insurance policy, take out, and will, in any event, keep up the premiums on such a policy, to provide the protection set out below, for a period of three years from the completion of the said work.

3. The policy to be taken out and kept up by the Contractor shall provide cover in respect of any legal liability which may result from the work carried out, under this agreement, by the Contractor, his servants or agents, in or in proximity to the said churchyard, in respect of injury to person or property, and in respect of loss or damage of any sort whatsoever thereby arising; and the Contractor agrees to indemnify the Incumbent and the PCC in respect of any claim which may be brought in respect of any such injury loss or damage.

4. The sum insured shall be to the extent of £................ (e) ....

5. The insurance policy stipulated in this agreement has been/will be (f) taken out with .... (g) .... of ....

6. The Contractor shall not be authorised to commence the work referred to in this agreement unless and until the said insurance policy is in force and shall be authorised to continue the work only as long as the said policy remains in force.

7. The Contractor shall, upon the request of the Incumbent or of the duly authorised representative of the PCC, produce for inspection the policy of insurance required under this agreement, and the receipts in respect of the payment of the current premium.

8. Before the work provided for in this agreement is begun the Contractor shall provide the Incumbent or the duly authorised representative of the PCC with a copy of the policy of insurance required under this agreement and of the receipts in respect of the current premium. (Note)

AS WITNESS   (Signatures of the parties)

DATE

NOTES

(a) Insert name of Parish.
(b) Insert name and address of Contractor.
(c) Insert location of churchyard.
(d) Set out details of the work. Where the work is specified in detail in an application to the incumbent for permission to erect a monument it is sufficient to refer to that application.
(e) Insert appropriate figure. It is suggested that this should be for a total of £1,000,000 in respect of any one incident.
(f) Delete as appropriate.
(g) Insert name and address of Contractor's insurers.
Note: Where a Contractor regularly carries out work in a particular churchyard it will normally only be necessary for a copy of the policy to be provided once and for a receipt of payment of premiums to be provided annually. Where contractors' insurance companies provide annual certificates as evidence of current insurance cover, it should be a simple procedure for the incumbent to keep a file of photocopies of current certificates and to request that a new one should be sent to him each year by each contractor who regularly carries out work in the churchyard.

Model Index-Card for Recording Burials in a Churchyard

(as used at Penn, Bucks)

Date of Death   Age   Date of Burial   Burial Reg. No.

(1)

(2)

Names and Addresses   Relationship

Next of Kin:

Family:

Memorial   Plot   Grave No.

Guild: Ann. Sub.   Cov.   Upkeep in Perpetuity

Solicitor

Bankers

Executor

APPENDIX V

Model Grave or Memorial Recording Form

	Denomination
	Graveyard/Cemetery
	Place
Dedication	Grid Ref
Recorder	Memorial No
Date of recording	Site grid ref
	Orientation
Inscription	Condition
	Height
	Width
	Thickness
	Materials
	Memorial Type
	Techniques of inscr
	Letter styles
	Dec motifs
	Languages
	Biblical quote
	Other quoted comment
	Anthropological terms
	Introductory term
	Occupations
	Mason & location
	People mentioned (not commem) M/F/?
	People commem
Photograph Neg no	Location of residence
	Location of body if elsewhere
	Comments
	Field check Base check

GRAVEYARDS CODE-SHEET

Labels on sheet	Codes	Meaning
CONDITION	A	Sound, *in situ*
(of stone)	B	Sound, displaced
(box 1)	C	Leaning or falling apart
	D	Collapsed
	E	Overgrown
CONDITION	A	Mint
(of inscription)	B	Clear
(box 2)	C	Mainly decipherable
	D	Traces
	E	Illegible/destroyed
MATERIALS	A	Slate
	B	White marble
	C	Grey marble
	D	Black marble
	E	Pink granite
	F	Grey granite
	G	Black granite
	H	Sandstone
	I	Brick
	J	Iron
	K	Basalt
	L	Concrete
	M	Limestone
	N	Brass
	O	Other
MEMORIAL TYPE	A	Flat
	B	Head
	C	Cross
	D	Tomb
	E	Foot
	F	Marked plot
	G	Body stone
	H	Wall plaque
	I	Effigy
	J	Pillar/obelisk
	K	Other

GRAVEYARDS CODE-SHEET

Labels on sheet	*Codes*	*Meaning*
TECHNIQUES OF	A	Incised
INSCRIPTION	B	Inlaid
	C	Relief
	D	Painted
LETTER STYLES	A	Italic
	B	Serif
	C	Sans serif
	D	Gothic
	E	Other
DECORATIVE MOTIFS	A	Bible
	B	Cross
	C	Death's head
	D	Cherub
	E	Urn
	F	Willow
	G	Hour glass
	H	Vine
	I	Pick and shovel
	J	Crossbones
	K	Columns and pediment
	L	Flowers
	M	Animals
	N	Ivy
	O	Leaves
	P	Birds
	Q	Scrollwork
	R	Fan
	S	Trefoil
	T	Fleur-de-lys
	U	Circles
	V	Ropework
	W	IHS
	X	Shield
	Y	Hands
	Z	Other

Directory of Useful Organisations

GENERAL

Council for the Care of Churches:
83 London Wall, London EC2M 5NA (01-638 0971)

Commonwealth War Graves Commission:
2 Marlow Road, Maidenhead, Berkshire SL6 7DX (0628 34221)

Historic Buildings and Monuments Commission for England (English Heritage):
Fortress House, 23 Savile Row, London W1X 2HE (01-734 6010)

Council for British Archaeology:
112 Kennington Road, London SE11 6RE (01-582 0494)

The National Association of Decorative and Fine Arts Societies (NADFAS):
30 Ebury Street, London SW1W 0LU (01-730 3041)

PLANNING AND DESIGN

Department of the Environment:
2 Marsham Street, London SW1 (01-212 3434)

Institute of Landscape Architects:
Nash House, Carlton House Terrace, London SW1 (01-839 4044)

LEGAL

The Home Office:
50 Queen Anne's Gate, London SW1 (01-213 3000)

The Legal Advisory Commission of the General Synod:
Church House, Great Smith Street, London SW1P 3NZ (01-222 9011)

National Association of Monumental Masons:
Crown Buildings, High Street, Aylesbury, Buckinghamshire
(0296 34750)

Memorial Advisory Bureau:
139 Kensington High Street, London W8 6SX (01-937 0052)

NATURE CONSERVATION

Royal Society for Nature Conservation (RSNC) and Watch Trust for
Environmental Education:
22 The Green, Nettleham, Lincoln LN2 2NR

The RSNC is the umbrella body for the forty-seven local Nature
Conservation Trusts. To promote the aims of conservation through
education the RSNC sponsors the WATCH Club for schools, families
and individual children. The RSNC will supply a list of all the local
Nature Conservation Trusts.

British Trust for Conservation Volunteers:
36 St Mary's Street, Wallingford, Oxford OX10 0EU (0491 39766)
BTCV (who will gladly supply a list of the regional offices) provides
advice, projects and training courses for groups and individuals wishing
to undertake practical conservation work. There are over 300 affiliated
local groups of volunteers who undertake regular tasks by request and
BTCV publishes a series of practical handbooks and training leaflets.

Nature Conservancy Council:
Northminster House, Peterborough PE1 1UA (0703 40345)
The Nature Conservancy Council is the government body which
promotes nature conservation in Great Britain. It gives advice on nature
conservation to government and all those whose activities affect our
wildlife and wild places. It also selects, establishes and manages a series
of National Nature Reserves. This work is based on detailed ecological
research and survey.
A range of publications is produced by the Interpretive Services Branch
and a catalogue listing current titles is available.

> East Anglia Region:
> 60 Bracondale, Norwich, Norfolk NR1 2BE (0603 620558)
> East Midlands Region:
> Northminster House, Peterborough PE1 1UA (0733 40345)
> North-East Region:
> Archbold House, Archbold Terrace, Newcastle upon Tyne NE2
> 1EG (091 2816316)
> North-West Region:
> Blackwell, Bowness-on-Windermere, Windermere, Cumbria LA23
> 3JR (09662 5286)

South Region:
Foxhold House, Thornford Road, Crookham Common, Newbury, Berkshire RG15 8EL (0635 238881)
South-East Region:
Zealds, Church Street, Wye, Ashford, Kent TN25 5BW (0233 812525)
South-West Region:
Roughmoor, Bishop's Hull, Taunton, Somerset TA1 5AA (0823 83211)
West Midlands Region:
Attingham Park, Shrewsbury, Shropshire SY4 4TW (0743 7761)

Fauna and Flora Preservation Society:
C/o Zoology Society of London, Regents Park, London NW1 4RY
Promotes the conservation of endangered species at home and abroad, and can supply a list of 'county bat groups or other contacts' for bats. There is also a list of county recorders and local groups for reptiles and amphibians.

Botanical Society of the British Isles:
C/o Department of Botany, British Museum (Natural History), Cromwell Road, London SW7 5BD
Members of the society are responsible for recording the flowering plants and ferns of the British Isles on a systematic basis and the production of an atlas for distribution.

British Lichen Society:
C/o British Museum (Natural History), Cromwell Road, London SW7 5BD
Concerned for the conservation of lichens, more particularly the rarer species found on many gravestones. Reprinting available on *Lichens in Churchyards* by F. H. Brightman and J. R. Laundon.

Council for Environmental Conservation:
London Ecology Centre, 80 York Way, London N1 9AG
The Council for Environmental Conservation is an independent national charity which co-ordinates the involvement of voluntary organisations in the United Kingdom in current environmental issues. It has an information service and produces a range of publications including a monthly newsletter *Habitat* and a quarterly newsheet *Habitat Digest*.

The Conservation Trust:
C/o George Palmer School, Northumberland Avenue, Reading, Berkshire RG2 7PW (0734 868442)

The Conservation Trust provides information on most environmental and conservation matters. Some of the services offered include: computer-assisted information services, resource bank of teaching materials, termly newsletter about environmental education and new publications, study notes and posters on popular environmental topics.

Countryside Commission:
John Dower House, Crescent Place, Cheltenham, Gloucestershire
GL50 3RA (0240 521281)

The Countryside Commission is the government's advisory and promotional body, with a duty to conserve the landscape beauty of England and Wales. It encourages the development and improvement of facilities for recreation, enjoyment and access in the countryside.

OTHER SPECIALIST SOCIETIES WHICH MIGHT GIVE ADVICE:

British Bryological Society (mosses and liverworts)

British Herpetological Society (reptiles and amphibia)

British Mycological Society (fungi)

Conchological Society of Great Britain (molluscs)

Royal Entomological Society (insects)

Addresses of the current secretaries for these societies may be obtained by writing to:
British Museum (Natural History), Cromwell Road, London SW7 5BD

Bibliography

GENERAL, INCLUDING HISTORICAL AND ARCHAEOLOGICAL

Philippe Aries	*The Hour of Our Death*. Penguin, 1983
Brian Bailey	*Churchyards of England and Wales*. Robert Hale, 1987
Frederick Burgess	*English Churchyard Memorials* (1969). Paperback edition SPCK, 1979
Pamela Burgess	*Churchyards*. SPCK, 1980
Camden History Society	*Buried in Hampstead: a survey of monuments at St John at Hampstead*. 1986
Mark Child	*Discovering Churchyards*. Shire Books, 1985
Church in Wales	*Report of the Archbishop of Wales's Commission on the Regulations for the Administration of Churchyards*. 1983
Edward L. Cutts	*An Essay on Church Furniture and Decoration*. Crockford, 1854
William Durandus	*The Symbolism of Churches and Church Ornaments:* a translation of the first book of the *Rationale Divinorum Officiorum* with an introductory essay and notes by John Mason Neale and Benjamin Webb. T. W. Green, 1843
Richard A. Etlin	*The Architecture of Death*. MIT Press, 1984
W. Hastings Kelke	*The Churchyard Manual, intended chiefly for rural districts*. C. Cox, 1851
Kenneth Lindley	*Graves and Graveyards*. Routledge and Kegan Paul, 1972
Hugh Meller	*London Cemeteries: an illustrated guide and gazetteer*. 2nd edition Gregg International, 1985

Richard Morris — *The Church in British Archaeology* (CBA research report, 47). Council for British Archaeology, 1983

Painswick Parochial Church Council — *Painswick Churchyard Tomb Trail: parts I and II* [n.d.]

Hermione Sandwith and Sheila Stainton — *The National Trust Manual of Housekeeping.* Allen Lane, 1984
Sculptural Memorials and Headstones. Sculpture Centre, 1938

Ben Stocker — *Medieval Grave Markers in Kent* in Church Monuments: journal of the Church Monuments Society, volume 1, part 2, 1986

NATURE CONSERVATION, INCLUDING MAINTENANCE

G. M. A. Barker — *Wildlife Conservation in the Care of Churches and Churchyards.* Church Information Office, 1977 (out of print; photocopies obtainable from CCC)

British Railways Board — *The Management of Lineside Vegetation: a guide to good practice.* 1985
The Care of Old Burial Grounds. Architectural Heritage Society of Scotland, Highland Group, 1987

A. R. Clapham, T. G. Tutin and E. F. Warburg — *Excursion Flora of the British Isles.* 3rd edition Cambridge University Press, 1981

Vaughan Cornish — *The Churchyard Yew and Immortality.* Frederick Muller, 1946

Francesca Greenoak — *God's Acre: the flowers and animals of the parish churchyard.* W. I. Books, 1985

D. L. Hawksworth and D. J. Hill — *The Lichen-Forming Fungi.* Blackie, 1984

F. Nigel Hepper — *Bible Plants at Kew.* HMSO, 1981

F. Nigel Hepper — *Planting a Bible Garden.* HMSO, 1987

Hans Martin Jahus — *Collins Guide to the Ferns, Mosses and Lichens of Britain and Northern and Central Europe.* Collins, 1980

David Macdonald — *Running with the Fox.* Unwin Hyman, 1987

W. Keble Martin	*The Concise British Flora in Colour.* Ebury Press/Michael Joseph, 1965; Sphere Books, 1972
Alan Mitchell	*A Field Guide to the Trees of Britain and Northern Europe.* Collins, 1974
Tony Mitchell-Jones	*Bats in Churches.* CCC, 1987
David Richardson	*The Vanishing Lichens: their history, biology and importance.* David and Charles, 1975
Francis Rose	*The Wild Flower Key: British Isles and N.W. Europe.* Frederick Warne, 1981
Mark R. D. Seaward (Ed)	*Lichen Ecology.* Academic Press, 1977
R. E. Stebbings and D. J. Jeffries	*Focus on Bats, their Conservation and the Law.* Nature Conservancy Council, 1982
	Wildlife Conservation in Essex Churchyards. (Sponsored by the Botanical Society of the British Isles, Essex County Council Planning Committee and Lynfield Motors Ltd of Witham, Essex) 1987

LETTERING AND CALLIGRAPHY

William Gardner	*Alphabet at Work.* Adam and Charles Black, 1982
Richard Grasby	*An Introduction to the Study and Classification of Lettering on Memorials.* 1983 (Obtainable from National Association of Decorative and Fine Arts Societies, 38 Ebury Street, London SW1W 0LU)
Michael Harvey	*Carving Letters in Stone and Wood.* Bodley Head, 1987
David Kindersley and Lida Lopes Cardozo	*Letters Slate Cut.* Lund Humphries, 1981

CONCERN FOR THE DYING AND BEREAVED

| June Benn | *Memorials: an anthology of poetry and prose.* Ravette, 1986 |
| Gilbert Cope (Ed) | *Dying, Death and Disposal.* SPCK, 1970 |

D. J. Enright (Ed)	*The Oxford Book of Death.* Oxford University Press, 1987
	Funerals and Ministry to the Bereaved: a handbook of funeral practices and procedures. Church House Publishing, 1985
Claire Gittings	*Death, Burial and the Individual in Early Modern England.* Croom Helm, 1984
John Hinton	*Dying.* Penguin, 1971
Richard Huntington and Peter Metcalf	*Celebrations of Death: the anthropology of mortuary ritual.* Cambridge University Press, 1979
John Hinton	*Dying.* Penguin, 1971
Richard Huntington and Peter Metcalf	*Celebrations of Death: the anthropology of mortuary ritual.* Cambridge University Pres, 1979
Edgar N. Jackson	*The Many Faces of Grief.* SCM Press, 1978
Elisabeth Kubler-Ross	*Living with Death and Dying.* Souvenir Press, 1982
Elisabeth Kubler-Ross	*On Death and Dying.* Tavistock, 1972
Richard Lamerton	*Care of the Dying.* Revised edition Penguin, 1980
C. S. Lewis	*A Grief Observed* (1961): Paperback edition Faber, 1966
Murray Parkes	*Bereavement.* Penguin, 1970
Lily Pincus	*Death and the Family: the importance of mourning.* Faber, 1974
John Prickett (Ed)	*Death.* Lutterworth, 1980
Dame Cicely Saunders (Ed)	*Beyond All Pain: a companion for the suffering and bereaved.* SPCK, 1983
P. Speck	*Loss and Grief in Medicine.* Bailliere Tindall, 1978
P. Speck and I. Ainsworth-Smith	*Letting Go: care of the dying and bereaved.* SPCK, 1982

LAW

For the main statutory materials and for detailed commentary:

Halsbury's	*Laws of England.* 4th edition Volume 10: *Cremation and Burial;* Volume 14: *Ecclesiastical Law* Butterworth

Halsbury's
Statutes. 4th edition Volume 5: *Burial and Cremation;* Volume 14: *Ecclesiastical Law* Butterworth

Encyclopaedia of Planning Law. 4 volumes Sweet and Maxwell (Loose-leaf, updated 3 times a year)

Canons of the Church of England. 4th edition Church House Publishing, 1987

The Opinions of the Legal Advisory Commission of the General Synod of the Church of England. 6th edition Church House Publishing, 1985

OTHER SPECIALIST WORKS

M. R. Russell Davies
The Law of Burial, Cremation and Exhumation. 5th edition Shaw, 1982

Kenneth M. Macmorran, and others
A Handbook for Churchwardens and Parochial Church Councillors. Revised edition Mowbray, 1986

E. Garth Moore and T. Briden
Introduction to English Canon Law. 2nd edition Mowbray, 1985

A general introduction covering the main relevant aspects of secular law:

J. D. S. Harte
Landscape, Land Use, and the Law. Spon, 1985